DAYTON GHOSTS & LEGENDS

SARA KAUSHAL

Haunted America

Published by Haunted America
A division of The History Press
Charleston, SC
www.historypress.com

Unless otherwise noted, all images are author photos.

First published 2023

Manufactured in the United States

ISBN 9781467154123

Library of Congress Control Number: 2023934791

Notice: The information in this book is true and complete to the best of our knowledge. It is offered without guarantee on the part of the author or The History Press. The author and The History Press disclaim all liability in connection with the use of this book.

To Shannon
Gone, but not forgotten

CONTENTS

ACKNOWLEDGEMENTS

I'd like to start by thanking my husband, Ravi, for all the support while I've been writing. For every author talk I had for *Murder & Mayhem in Dayton and the Miami Valley*, you were there to encourage me, to be a familiar face in the crowd and to give me honest feedback. Ravi, you're my number one person, and I am so grateful to have you in my life.

To Tim Sikora and Randy "Diva" Lake, I thank you both for helping me get a better understanding of the aircrafts I've mentioned in the Wright-Patterson chapter. Without your help, that chapter would have been much shorter and less informative.

Thank you to Martha Ballinger from Dayton Metro Library, who has helped me schedule author talks and with research for Dayton Unknown for years. Thank you to Kris Lininger from Wright Library, for suggesting the subject for a presentation, which led to this book. Librarians are the best!

Thank you to my friends and family on Facebook who shared stories and weighed in on the type of stories you wanted to read. Thank you also for all the support you've given with author talks and publicity.

INTRODUCTION

When it comes to real estate, it's all about location. Perhaps it is the same for supernatural real estate in the Dayton area. Regarding otherworldly or unexplained phenomena, here's how our little section of the world makes big waves:

Bellbrook is considered Ohio's "Sleepy Hollow."
Ohio is eighth in the nation for UFO sightings (4,234). Dayton is a significant city for UFO sightings.
Ohio is fourth in the nation for Bigfoot sightings.
Ohio is on the Travel Channel's top-ten list for Bigfoot sightings worldwide.
Miamisburg holds the record for the most sightings of a ghost in one location.
Germantown is the "mecca for Dogman sightings."
Bellbrook is supposedly on the migratory path for Bigfoot.
Yellow Springs has a large number of reported hauntings, and it's theorized there's a vortex of energy in the town attracting the supernatural. The iron-rich, yellowish-orange spring is considered the center of the vortex.

When I say I've read just about everything there is on ghost stories in the Dayton area, it's no understatement. Before doing research for this book, I knew a lot of these stories already. But I gathered more information and learned so many new stories as well. While writing this book, I did many of my favorite things all at once. I researched, I wrote and I got to read ghost stories.

As you read this book, you may notice the stories included are not located on private property and do not involve recent deaths. This is intentional. In some cases, the names of people involved are known but have been changed or not included to give those involved and their surviving family members privacy.

Some of my stories involve details obtained from personal recollections or from stories that circulated in the Dayton area as I grew up. I have very few personal experiences with ghosts and the supernatural other than stories I've heard. I blame this partly on my own skepticism. I'm always trying to find a tangible explanation for such events, but it doesn't mean I don't believe. For me, I just seem to find explanations too often. This doesn't stop my imagination from running wild, though!

On this note, I should mention that in many cases, the details of these stories don't line up any particular place or known event in the Dayton area. Some of these are simply stories that are shared, not necessarily based in provable events. Stories that circulate by word of mouth take on a life of their own!

I do have one tidbit to share. I'm not sure how to categorize this, but it has happened too often and for too many years for me to consider it a coincidence anymore.

I have a song that forewarns me of death. Before someone I know dies, I will hear "The Middle" by Jimmy Eat World. I usually hear it once after as well. The most recent time I heard it was the day before an aunt died and again on the way home from her funeral. This has been happening since 2002, when a coworker at my job died. I heard the song on the radio on the way home, just after I learned of his death. One week later, I heard the song again on the way home from work, and then I learned of a classmate's death. This pattern has continued for every loss I've experienced and continues today. I used to attribute this "death song" to the popularity of the song, but as the song gets older, it's played less often on the radio. But it will still pop up randomly just before I learn of a loved one's death. I think the song is a way to send comfort. The lyrics include the following:

> *It just takes some time*
> *Little girl, you're in the middle of the ride*
> *Everything, everything'll be just fine*
> *Everything, everything'll be alright, alright.*

I hope you enjoy the stories, put any skepticism away, and believe while you read, because whether you believe in ghosts or not, they certainly believe in you.

1

DAYTON'S BLESSING FROM THE WATERVLIET SHAKERS

Located along County Line Road and Research Boulevard in Kettering and Beavercreek (the county line separating Greene and Montgomery Counties) was once a Shaker village named Watervliet. The Shakers were followers of Mother Ann Lee, who came from Manchester, England, and established the first Shaker community in Watervliet, New York. This religious sect believed in communal living, celibacy, and public confession of sins. As this was not a community repopulated by procreation, it relied solely on converts for its citizenry. Due to declining population, a large group of Shakers moved to Ohio on a missionary trip to seek out new converts. They established communities in several areas, including Dayton and Lebanon. Lebanon had one of the largest Shaker populations. Many new members were homeless or migrant workers who joined in the winter for food and shelter then left once the weather got warm. When winter came around again, they reconverted. The Shakers never turned them away, but this certainly did not contribute to or increase the sect's population. The Shakers had to continue seeking converts from other religions.

In Dayton, the Shaker community recruited from a nearby Presbyterian community in the Beavercreek area called Beulah. Many of the community members were already dissatisfied with their faith, so the transition was easy. The rest of Dayton left the Shakers alone for the most part and let them live their lives unperturbed.

Lebanon, however, did not like the Shakers living in their area. The Shaker branch located there did not have the same experience as their

Marker commemorating the location of the Watervliet Shaker Community.

Dayton counterparts. Frustrated with the conversion attempts by the Shakers, residents of Lebanon antagonized the sect with fires and vandalism on their property and violent attacks on individual Shakers and groups when they were separated from the community. The majority of the agitators were disgruntled preachers from other faiths. In 1810, a group of residents invaded the Lebanon Shaker settlement, known as Union Village. The mob found no signs of injustice or cruelty, so they dispersed and left the village without harming any property or person.

In 1820, a Shaker brother had a heavenly vision telling him that Lebanon should be cursed and Dayton blessed. One day, groups of Shakers marched up and down the streets of Lebanon, shouting, "Woe on all persecutors." Later in the day, in an act of gratitude for Dayton's more welcoming environment, two men from the Shaker community rode into Dayton and shouted, "Blessings on all kindly souls," intended for the community of Dayton and its people.

Perhaps it is a coincidence, but while both cities had roughly 1,000 people in 1820, by 1840, Dayton had grown to 6,067 and Lebanon was at 1,327. By 1890, Dayton's population was 61,220 and Lebanon's was 3,174. Today, Dayton is still the more populated city.

The wrath of the Shakers may extend beyond the curse they uttered in Lebanon that day. As Jane* was visiting the Watervliet Shaker House at Carillon Historical Park, her husband made a few remarks making fun of the Shaker lifestyle and calling their sexual beliefs crazy. After her husband, their fifteen-year-old and the rest of the tour group went outside, Jane and her seventeen-year-old daughter remained inside to look around a bit more. As Jane walked down the steps, a large rock flew across the floor. Jane picked it up, not wanting it to get kicked around and scratch the floor. As she was leaning forward to grab it, her daughter came flying into her, knocking them both into the door. The daughter said she was shoved down the steps. Jane believed her, as her daughter did not fall but moved forward over the steps. They quickly went outside and caught up to their family and asked them why they didn't remain inside with them. They replied that something felt weird inside. Maybe the Shakers didn't like hearing jokes about their beliefs and tried to teach the family a lesson.

Although the Shakers eventually dissipated, Dayton has honored them by naming two streets after them, Shakertown Road and Watervliet Avenue.

---

*Name changed at request of witness.

2
GHOSTLY GRAVEYARDS

GERMANTOWN CEMETERY

The ghost of a Civil War soldier is said to wander around the cemetery. He is believed to be a Confederate soldier who died while separated from his company. The caretaker's house in the cemetery is also haunted, but by a different ghost. This ghost has a malignant presence and likes to slam doors. Windows open and shut on their own, and the spirit likes to pace back and forth across the upstairs room, often stomping.

WOLFE CEMETERY

Established as a family cemetery, the Wolfe Cemetery in Centerville started with the burial of Rhoda Wolfe in 1845. As the years went by, the only people buried in the cemetery were those either born or married into the family, with one exception: Wilson Patrick, a hired hand with no family. A witch or warlock was buried in the cemetery as well, indicated by a grave marker with a flat top. If you lie on it or touch it, you can feel the heat from the stone and can potentially get sucked into the grave. Another legend is that one member of the Wolfe family had pet wolves and wanted to be buried with the animals. The wolves were buried alive with their owner. Their ghosts can be seen roaming the cemetery and have been heard howling and scratching from underground.

WILLOW VIEW CEMETERY

The witch's grave.

Willow View Cemetery was established in 1897 over an existing cemetery, known as Union Cemetery (also called Beardshear Cemetery or the Old Beardshear Church Cemetery). The cemetery stretches along both sides of Wagner Ford Road. Willow View is said to be home to the grave of a witch. As the story goes, Sophia Thiele, reputed to be a witch, died in 1897. The church refused to give her a proper Christian burial, instead burying her next to an old stump outside the church. Members of her family came along after dark and hung a wooden sign with her name on it over the stump. The next morning, the pastor arrived to find the stump, the sign and the rope used to hang the sign all had turned to stone. If you find yourself in the cemetery during a full moon, lay your hand on top of the stone. You will feel the stone sink into the ground.

HILLGROVE CEMETERY

When Hillgrove Cemetery in Miamisburg was established in 1863, it was decided that the burials of nearby Village Cemetery would be moved there. This process took a long time, nearly twenty years, to complete. While many of the families delayed moving bodies, some families simply moved the headstones to the new cemetery, left the bodies and called it a day. The final push to move the bodies from Village Cemetery is explained in the Library Park story in chapter 11.

Eventually, the other cemeteries in the area were no longer being used, and Hillgrove's rolling hills became the primary location for Miamisburg's burials. Today, the Hillgrove Union Cemetery Board provides oversight to Hillgrove Cemetery. The grounds are open daily except during periods of inclement weather.

Walking through Hillgrove, one might encounter the spirit of a young girl sitting on a grave, crying her eyes out. It is said she sits at her mother's grave. Approach her if you dare, but if you speak to her, she will not reply. She will simply look at you, then disappear. She is not alone haunting the cemetery. The crying ghost has a nineteen-year-old companion, the daughter of a preacher. Her father believed strongly in his teachings, and when he discovered that his daughter did not believe the same, he disowned her. Devastated, she used a knife to commit suicide. The stone Bible on her grave will look broken at a glance, but in the blink of an eye it will look perfectly fine again.

WOODLAND CEMETERY

Woodland Cemetery is one of the oldest garden cemeteries in the United States and one of the older cemeteries in the Dayton area. There are over two hundred acres of trees, hills, native plants and, of course, gravestones. Many famous people are among the one hundred thousand burials in Woodland. The Wright brothers, Erma Bombeck, Paul Laurence Dunbar and Charles F. Kettering (located in the mausoleum) are just a few.

Johnny Morehouse

Johnny Morehouse is more well known in death than he was in life. He was the youngest son of a cobbler and lived an unassuming life in the back of the shop at the southwest corner of Third and June Streets, along the Dayton Canal. On August 14, 1860, five-year-old Johnny was playing near the Miami and Erie Canal (now Patterson Boulevard) in front of his home and, somehow, fell in the canal and drowned.

There are three popular theories of why Johnny's gravestone depicts him with his dog. In the first version, the dog jumped in after Johnny to rescue him and they both drowned. The toys depicted in stone on the grave are the toys found in Johnny's pockets when he was pulled out of the canal. According to the second version, Johnny's dog loved him so much that he wouldn't leave his grave. Visitors to Johnny's grave would bring water and scraps of food for the dog. When he eventually died, the monument was erected to honor his devotion to Johnny. The third and most likely version of the story is simply that Johnny loved his dog and that his grieving parents opted for a monument to reflect the love between a boy and his dog.

Johnny Morehouse's tombstone. Visitors regularly leave toys for Johnny and treats for his dog.

Friends of the Morehouse family interviewed in the 1890s stated that the monument simply demonstrates the love between a boy and his dog. Descendants of the Morehouse family have not been able to confirm any version of the story and newspaper accounts were not written to tell the tale. When Johnny died in 1860, only a short, one-sentence announcement appeared in the paper, announcing his name, age, his parents' names and date of his death. The death announcement, found in the *Dayton Journal* of August 17, 1860, simply states he died on August 14, age four years and eleven months, and that he was the youngest son of John N. and Mary M. Morehouse.

Some accounts of Johnny's death state he froze to death in the water. In the heat of August, that was simply not possible. Historical weather data shows that temperatures did not dip low enough in August 1860 for Johnny to freeze to death in the water.

Although the stories of his death made him popular, the stories of his afterlife made Johnny famous. Witnesses living near or walking near Woodland Cemetery after dark have reported seeing a young boy walking along the paths of the cemetery with a dog, sometimes playing fetch. The dog joyfully barks and plays alongside his companion. In June 1997, a man sitting on his porch spotted a young boy and his dog walking through the cemetery after dark. The boy was wearing old-fashioned clothing. He seemed too young to be alone, but it was obvious to the man that this little boy did not have an adult with him. He sent his grandson into the cemetery to go get the boy, but his grandson returned alone. He did not see any signs of the boy in the cemetery when he walked around. The man called the Dayton Police, and a massive search ensued. After not finding the young boy by a ground search, they organized a helicopter search using infrared technology that reacts to heat sources. If a living boy and his dog were walking there, heat traces would have been detected. But none were found.

If you visit Johnny's marble tombstone, which stands prominently at about five feet tall, you'll see coins, toys and dog treats left by visitors as a sign of respect. Put your hand up to the dog's nose, and you'll feel air on your hand, as if he is still breathing.

The Crying Girl

Another popular tale of Woodland Cemetery is the young girl who cries while sitting on top of a grave. She's described as having blond hair and blue eyes and wearing blue jeans, white sneakers, a red shirt and a dark blue sweater tied around her waist. Many who have seen her say she was crying too hard to have a conversation or to be aware of those around her. Others have reported having short conversations with her, not knowing she was dead. She normally sits on a tombstone, but nobody has ever gotten the name from it. One visitor to Woodland reported talking to her, but she didn't respond, she just cried. As the visitor drove away from the cemetery, he could still hear the crying in his car. Many believe she cries because she and her father are buried at separate ends of the cemetery. A trio of college students walking through the cemetery after dark saw a young girl crying profusely on the steps in front of a mausoleum. When they asked her if she needed help, she stood up, stretched out her arms and floated backward into the closed doors of the mausoleum without saying a word.

Glowing Tombstone

Marycrest Hall on the University of Dayton campus runs along the border of Woodland's newer section of gravestones. Known affectionately as the "Crest," it is the largest residential facility on campus. From their windows, many residents on the north side can see into the cemetery. Reports of a glowing tombstone have come in many times over the years. Some believe it's the tombstone belonging to the crying girl; others believe it's a different haunting entirely.

The Little Girl

The ghost of a little girl appears to visitors who hang out around the entrance. Most of the sightings are brief but memorable. In one instance, a husband and wife were looking at some old tombstones not far from the entrance when a little girl playing near the fence approached and asked if they needed help finding anything. The couple still remembers how off-putting it was to see such a young girl playing unattended. Another couple walking the cemetery just before it closed saw the same young girl standing near the gates at the entrance. As they walked back to their car, the girl told them they should head home, that this was not the place they should be. Just then, a gust of wind blew through the fall air, and in an instant, the girl had vanished in a swirl of leaves.

Sealed Vault

The holding vault was an aboveground tomb originally used to store coffins during times when they could not be buried in the ground, such as when the ground was too muddy or frozen. In some cases, the vault held a body until friends and relatives could be there to attend the funeral, such as with Matilda Stanley, "Queen of the Gypsies." Matilda was so well loved that when she died in January 1878, her body was held until September to give friends and family from all over the world time to travel to Dayton to attend her funeral. Between fifteen thousand and twenty-five thousand attendees swarmed Woodland. Since the advent of power equipment to dig into the ground, the receiving vault is no longer necessary and sits unused.

It was a typical morning when a groundskeeper opening the cemetery gates heard screaming from the holding vault. Going over to investigate, he saw an older man inside. He had been wandering around drunk the night before and the next thing he knew, he woke up in the vault with no memory of how he got there. Workers had to use a torch to cut through the metal gates of the only entrance to get him out. The gates had rusted shut over time and from lack of use. To this day, nobody, including the man, knows how he got in there.

Paul Laurence Dunbar

Visitors to Woodland at dusk, especially in pleasant spring and summer weather, have spotted a man sitting atop a stone reciting poetry and telling stories. A closer look reveals it is the stone marking Paul Laurence Dunbar's grave and the reader is none other than the poet himself. Dunbar was buried beneath a willow tree, in honor of the engraving on his gravestone, which was written in the dialect of the American Black community in the late 1800s and early 1900s.

> *Lay me down beneath de willers in de grass*
> *Whah de branch'll go a-singin' as it pass*
> *An, w'en I's a-layin' low,*
> *I kin hyeah it as it go*
> *Singin', "Sleep, my honey, tek yo' res' at las."*

Other Ghosts

Other experiences not associated with specific graves or people have happened at Woodland. Conversations can be heard when nobody is around, tombstones fluctuate in temperature then change back within minutes, shadows move of their own accord and apparitions of soldiers have been seen wandering through the Civil War section. An unidentified young man has been seen walking around the cemetery at night but has not been near enough to a single grave to indicate who he might be. As you enter Woodland's main entrance, you will notice a bronze statue of a man sitting in a chair, the late businessman Adam Schantz. Schantz operated a brewery, a butcher shop and a water-purification system. Despite multiple tragedies that would have put others out of business, Schantz persevered and relied on his stellar reputation to rebuild his businesses. His ghost has been seen wandering the cemetery. Perhaps it's that persevering spirit still trying to rebuild after death. A former caretaker has been spotted as well, still tending to the grounds of Woodland Cemetery from beyond the grave.

FIFTH AND LUDLOW

An 1802 diagram of downtown Dayton, including the city's first cemetery, located at Fifth and Ludlow Streets. *Public domain.*

In downtown Dayton, the south side of Fifth Street between Wilkinson and Ludlow hides a secret. Daniel Cooper, one of the founders of Dayton, suggested four acres of land to be used as a cemetery. In 1805, what is now the corner of Fifth and Ludlow was selected for its use. As a result of population expansion and space becoming more valuable, the marked graves in the lot were moved to other cemeteries outside downtown in order to accommodate new construction.

Unfortunately, many burials were unmarked graves or poorly recorded, meaning most of the bodies were not exhumed when the cemetery was moved. For years, any construction done in that area unearthed more bodies. People walking near the intersection have heard odd sounds, felt cold spots and have even seen apparitions in the middle of the day. Businesses nearby have reported hauntings as well. Spaghetti Warehouse has experienced dishes thrown on the floor, the sound of whispers and even the sight of customers seating themselves at tables only to disappear moments later.

3

BIZARRE BEASTS

BUTTER STREET MONSTER

Although well known in the cryptid community, the stories of the Butter Street Monster are less known in Germantown and Dayton. If you ask a resident of Germantown, the answer will be on one of two ends of the spectrum—they either have heard of it as long as they can remember and can tell you stories, or they have never heard anything about it at all. It's known more commonly as the Butter Street Monster, as Butter Street was the location of the first few sightings, which started almost immediately after the street was created. The creature has also been called the Beast of Anthony Road, the Germantown Werewolf and its cryptid name, Dogman. In the Dogman community, Germantown is considered the mecca of Dogman sightings. The incidents have been going on for over sixty years, with confirmed sightings as recent as 2016. Sightings have dwindled in more recent years, as the land is more developed, with fewer places for a creature to hide.

The area of the sightings in Germantown centers on Germantown MetroPark. The majority of sightings are on Anthony Road and Butter Street. (Germantown MetroPark is located in the land between the roads.) On its 2,665 acres, Germantown MetroPark has ravines, trees, wildflowers, meadows and prairies, all of which would give any beast or creature the opportunity to live and to hide from humans. Also near the sightings are gravel pits, farms and several sources of water, making this area a great location for large creatures to dwell. In this area, there have been many reports of half-eaten animals and unidentified tracks that are attributed to the Butter Street Monster. There were a lot of sightings on Anthony Road. Jefferson Township Police built a facility on that road with several cameras and signs indicating that the cameras were watching anyone in the vicinity. Dogman experts believe this was to keep watch on the Dogman sightings in the area.

Butter Street was the location of the first sightings of the Butter Street Monster, giving the creature its name.

Witnesses have described the creature as bipedal and large, maybe ten feet tall with a shoulder span of four feet. The creature is covered with dark fur and has a terrifying howl that sounds like nothing they've heard before. Descriptions of the creature generally fall into one of two classifications: K9 Type and Type 3. The K9 Type looks like an upright canid (mammal of the dog family) with more doglike features and a tail. Generally, they are described looking similar to werewolves or large dogs. The Type 3 sightings describe a creature more like Bigfoot, with a dog's head and no tail, but instead of fingernails and toenails like Bigfoot, they have claws

Although many Dogman hunters start their searches at night, more sightings actually take place during the day. Many sightings have occurred while people are taking out their trash or simply coming home. The most important thing to know is that in all reported sightings of the Butter Street Monster, 99 percent of witnesses get away, scared but unharmed. Less than 1 percent of witnesses have been attacked or physically harmed. Many cryptozoologists and Dogman experts believe the Dogman is not dangerous to humans but only curious about them. One example of this curiosity occurred during the Halloween season, when the Land of Illusion Theme Park set up its Haunted Scream Park. One of the employees approached a man who was dressed in a werewolf costume near the edge of the park. When he got closer, he realized that it was not a human being. Both he and the creature ran away frightened. Regardless, if you plan to go hunting for the Butter Street Monster, be prepared to get away.

Thank you to Joedy Cook for information on sightings and history.

BIGFOOT IN GERMANTOWN

A sighting in 2005 of Bigfoot along Diamond Mill Road is just one of many. The witness and her husband were coming home from her mother's house in Middletown late one night when she spotted the creature crossing the street in front of them, illuminated by the car's headlights. As they were rounding the curve on Diamond Mill Road just after merging from Cherry Street, she witnessed a bipedal animal over six feet tall covered in dark hair. The creature was rusty brown and had a long stride when it walked. Her husband was driving and did not see it because he was focused on the curve in the road ahead. The witness shared the story with everyone she knew and learned a neighbor had seen a similar creature in the same stretch of road. A sighting similar to this was recorded by the Bigfoot Field Research Organization in 1988 on Eby Road, roughly a mile away. The BFRO noted several sources of food, water and shelter in the area that could support a large creature.

BOGGY CREEK MONSTER, KETTERING

A group of Kettering teenagers went camping one night in the 1950s alongside a creek in a large field. When they did not return home the next morning, their parents went looking for them. They found the campsite with embers still smoldering in the firepit. The kids were gone; no sign of them was ever found. Rumors circulated that a large creature attacked and killed the kids. The creature reportedly took its victims into the water before killing and eating them, thus leaving no trace. The creature was later given the nickname "Boggy Creek Monster" when the 1970s horror movie with that title came out. The monster itself was based on the Fouke Monster, which frightened residents of Fouke, Arkansas, in the 1960s. It stands to reason that there could have been more than one creature if it existed. To this day, noises sounding like a large and fast creature moving through the brush are still reported.

SEVEN DACHSHUNDS, YELLOW SPRINGS

Dave Dye didn't hesitate when an old German man appeared at his door asking for food. The man didn't give his name but seemed so exhausted that Dye didn't think twice before inviting him in for the night. The two shared a meal and beers while telling stories and talking all evening. The man told Dye he had come all the way from Germany that day. He was getting more agitated as the night advanced. Finally, he asked Dye if he had good locks on his door. Dye asked him if he was afraid of robbers. "No," the German replied, "dogs."

Dye himself was an avid dog lover and was surprised at this answer. He mentioned that he had a dog of his own, a greyhound. To this, the German replied that the dogs he was worried about were faster and said that they were dachshunds. Dye roared with laughter at this response, imagining the tiny dogs racing past his greyhound. Indignant, the German replied that he had killed a man in Germany and immediately took the first boat out of the country. The dead man's seven dogs followed him onto the boat, and he hadn't a moment's peace since. In the distance, the men heard the faint sound of dogs barking. Dye was still laughing at the story. The German retorted that he would fool the dogs that night. The pack barked and snarled outside Dye's home all night. In the morning, when Dye went to wake the old man, he was gone. It appeared he had climbed out of the second-story window. From there, he climbed into a tree, then presumably leaped onto a passing wagon heading out of town—all to elude the dogs tracking his scent. He was never seen again, but the dogs remained outside Dye's house for six nights before giving up on their target.

ZOMBIE DEER, GREENE COUNTY

Imagine going for a walk in the woods and encountering a deer crawling on its knees, drooling and panting. Zombie Deer, as they've been called, have been appearing in multiple counties in Ohio, including Greene County. Named for their unmoving stance and undead appearance, zombie deer symptoms include swelling, bleeding, patchy fur and loss of fear of humans. These "zombies" are often found near water, a result of their dehydration and fever. Although they have a supernatural moniker, these deer are affected with a scientifically explained illness called epizootic hemorrhagic disease (EHD). The disease is transmitted by biting midges, insects small as gnats that live in small pools of standing water.

THE CROSSWICK MONSTER

The small village of Crosswick, located north of Waynesville, is so small that only one road runs through it. It remained small and relatively unknown until May 1882, when two young boys, Ed and Joe Lynch, were fishing in a small creek known as Satterthwaites Run. As they sat along the bank, a large reptile-like creature slithered out from the trees toward the boys. The screams of both boys attracted three men, Reverend Jacob Horn, George Peterson and Allen Jordan, who came running toward the boys as the creature picked Ed up and attempted to run off with him. The startled creature dropped Ed, who was swiftly carried home. Dr. Lukens of Waynesville was summoned to care for him. Lukens later described Ed as terribly shaken and badly bruised and suffering from convulsions and spasms into the night. When Ed finally fell asleep, he awoke frequently in terror.

While Ed was getting medical treatment, sixty men set out on a mission to find the monster. Armed with clubs, guns, axes and hunting dogs, they first attacked the sycamore tree behind which it was spotted. The creature jumped out from its hiding spot and reared up on its hind legs. It ran terrified across the creek, through a field and then over a fence, breaking it. When it was first encountered, many of the men ran away, but the ones who remained pursued the creature until it found its hiding spot in the ground. The creature has been described as anywhere from twelve to forty feet long, with a diameter of sixteen inches. Its legs are four feet long, and the entire body is covered in scales. Its feet are about twelve inches long and shaped like a lizard's feet. The creature is black and white with large yellow spots. Its head is about sixteen inches wide. It has a long, black forked tongue and the inside of the mouth is a deep red.

BURIED GIANTS

Although these giant skeletons were determined to be a hoax by many sources, including the *Columbus Dispatch*, they persisted for decades. In articles dating from the mid-1800s to well into the early 1900s, reports of giant skeletons popped up all over the country. The skeletons were reported to be anywhere from seven to nine feet tall and prehistoric, and the bones were often found in caves or near sacred mounds. The Dayton area had its share of giant skeletons, many of which were reportedly those of mound builders. It was theorized that their larger bodies were better able perform the labor involved in building the mounds. A few of the "discoveries" are summarized here.

On January 14, 1899, while digging in a gravel pit a half mile from Miamisburg Mound, Edward Kauffman and Edward Gebhart found an oversized skull. Local experts were consulted and confirmed it to be from a prehistoric man. The skull had a gorilla-like angularity and a large jawbone. Examination of the teeth indicated that the person had been a vegetarian, and the man was calculated to be eight feet, one inch tall, larger than any known man at the time. The man was buried in a sitting position with knees drawn up to his chest.

On November 25, 1904, a skeleton was found in a gravel pit east of the city by owner W.C. Fry. The skeleton measured about nine feet in length and was estimated to be six times larger than the average man. Professors Metzler and Foerste of Steele High School believed that the bones were of a primeval race.

On August 12, 1905, a skeleton of oversized proportions was discovered in another gravel pit, but it could not be examined, as the remains were so old that they crumbled when exposed to the air. Only the jaw remained intact. Visible on the left side of the jaw was a one-inch tusk. Before the skeleton disintegrated, investigators were able to determine that it had been buried in a sitting position with its knees drawn up toward the chest. It had a long skull with some sort of cranial deformity. Attorney T.B. Herman was present when the skeleton was discovered and claimed it had no similarity to the skeletons of the mound builders.

4

DREADFUL DEATHS

Some deaths stand out from others. When a brutal death occurs, ghosts are not far behind. Maybe the ghost needs closure, or maybe the person's death was so horrible that they cannot yet move on.

BESSIE LITTLE

Bessie Little had a difficult life. She was adopted as a young toddler from an orphanage in Troy. When Peter and Elizabeth Little walked into the orphanage, a little girl named Tress Doty walked directly to Mrs. Little and reached her arms out to be picked up. Elizabeth was enamored and chose her instantly. They brought her home and renamed her Bessie. During Bessie's childhood, her parents always made sure to remind her that she was lucky they picked her to be their adopted daughter. Their attitude during her childhood was basically, "You're welcome." As soon as she was old enough, Bessie was sent to work to earn money for her parents as a domestic servant. Those who knew her described her as both sweet and beautiful.

Albert Frantz grew up in a different world. As the youngest of five children, Albert was spoiled not only by his wealthy parents but by his siblings as well. As an adult, Albert worked as a stenographer for the Mathias Planing Mill Company, making good money. Those who knew Albert described him as cruel and cunning, but Bessie didn't care. She was completely infatuated with him.

After her mother discovered her with Albert in the barn in yet another less than "lady-like" situation, Bessie was sent out on her own. Her mother gave her clear instructions: Don't come back until Albert agrees to marry you. Bessie's situation only became more troublesome when she realized she was pregnant. Albert paid for Bessie to stay in a boardinghouse but told her he could not marry her because his father did not approve of their relationship. Bessie was older than Albert, a situation that was uncommon for the time. Albert was not of the age to marry, so he would need his father's consent, which he did not have. Desperate for help, Bessie penned a letter to Albert's father in hopes he would change his mind. For reasons unknown, she did not send the letter. Bessie threatened to take legal action to force Albert to marry her but relented when he sweet-talked her.

Hoping to win his heart, Bessie continued to see Albert, although she confided in a friend that she suspected he wanted to get rid of her. On a date prior to that conversation, she saw a gun on the seat in the carriage. During that date, she noticed that Albert had reached for the gun several times but pulled his hand away, as if changing his mind. She suspected Albert wanted to use it to kill her but chickened out before doing so. On the night of August 27, 1892, she accompanied him for what she thought would be a romantic buggy ride. Instead, as the couple crossed the bridge over Ridge Avenue, Albert shot her twice in the head and pushed her body into the water below. Returning home without Bessie, Albert quickly wrote a letter to another woman, asking her to marry him. The next day, he burned his barn to the ground with his horse and buggy inside. He then went to Bessie's boardinghouse and paid for another week's rent. Her landlady told him that she hadn't returned. He reassured her that Bessie would come back soon.

A week later, a bather in the Stillwater River discovered a body floating in the water. In bad condition, the body was almost unrecognizable. Mrs. Freese, who owned the boardinghouse where Bessie stayed, recognized the description in the newspaper of the clothing worn by the body and identified Bessie to police. Her parents made a visual identification but refused to take the body for burial, stating Bessie had been dead to them when she left the home. Bessie was buried. Her cause of death was determined to be suicide, a result of being pregnant and Albert not marrying her. She didn't stay buried long, as public outcry caused Bessie to be dug up and reexamined. That's when two bullet holes were discovered in her head. Albert was promptly arrested. Before the trial, Bessie was dug up once again and decapitated. Her head was put into a large glass jar and used as evidence. During the trial, Albert's defense was that Bessie had shot herself, and in a panic, he threw her

Above: Bessie Little Bridge, located on Ridge Avenue.

Left: Bessie's head was removed from her body and put in a large jar for evidence in the trial. *Courtesy of Newspapers.com.*

body into the river. This story did not hold up, as one shot would have killed her instantly and the other would have paralyzed her. If that wasn't enough, the shock of being shot the first time would have rendered her unable to shoot herself again. With his defense torn to pieces, Albert was convicted and put to death. Due to a loose wire, it took five tries before Albert was successfully executed in the electric chair. After Albert's execution, Bessie was exhumed for the fourth and final time and moved to a plot in Woodland Cemetery, section 111.

Perhaps Bessie can't rest knowing how many people wronged her in her life. Visitors to the Ridge Avenue Bridge, also known as the Bessie Little Bridge, have spotted an ethereal woman wearing Victorian clothing gazing into the water. She does not speak or interact with anyone but just stares into the water then disappears. If one sits quietly, they might experience the last sounds Bessie heard before her death: her screams and two gunshots. After that, a splash in the water below.

Those with triskaidekaphobia (fear of the number thirteen) might be interested in the article published in the *Xenia Daily Gazette* of January 27, 1897, which notes Albert Frantz's connection to the number thirteen in detail.

Albert was thirteen years of age when his mother died on the 13th of the month. His name contains thirteen letters; the name of his victim, Bessie R. Little, contains thirteen letters; the name of his attorney, in whom he confided, John W. Kreitzer, contains thirteen letters; he conveyed his sweetheart to the scene of her tragic death with a horse and buggy; which is spelled out with thirteen letters, his trial continued thirteen days and the sentence (electrocution) which he received contains thirteen letters, and to crown all, his death is fixed for the thirteenth day of May.

MURDER IN FROGTOWN

Take a walk down Dayton Street until you strike mud and you are in Frogtown. Frogtown was considered to be legally part of Yellow Springs, but not everything that went on there was legal. Frogtown had a reputation as a hangout for less than savory characters.

It was 1892, and one of the more well-known residents of Frogtown was pretty little Lou Keys. Lou had an eye for a good-looking fellow, a widower and father of three, George Koogler. When George put on his military uniform, there was no denying he was a handsome man. Passersby could hear him singing his favorite song, "My Pretty Quadroon," to Lou in his rich baritone voice as they walked arm in arm to her place.

> *I'll never forget when I met sweet Cora, my pretty quadroon*
> *I see her dear eyes shining yet as we vowed to be true 'neath the moon*
> *Her form was exceedingly fair, she had cheeks like the wild rose in June*
> *And the ringlets of dark glossy hair were the curls of my pretty quadroon*

Yellow Springs resident Andy Huntster also had eyes for Lou. Andy was listed in the 1880 census as an "imbecile" and worked in the restaurant owned by his father, Edward Huntster. When Lou was kind to him, Andy mistook her kindness for flirtation and was especially heartbroken when George won Lou's heart. Jealousy gripped Andy whenever he saw George and Lou walk by the restaurant with linked arms. It was especially difficult for him the night the couple ate oysters at his father's restaurant. They were noticed especially for the good time they were having that night, drinking until tipsy, flirting with each other shamelessly and staying out until 11:00 p.m. They were last seen walking arm in arm toward Lou's frame shanty in Frogtown.

The next morning, a neighbor found George splayed on the sidewalk in front of Lou's house. His pockets had been emptied and his pension money, which he had picked up the day before, was missing.

Inside the house lying near the door was Lou. Sadly, she didn't look so pretty anymore. Someone had attacked the couple with a hatchet and split open their skulls. An ice pick had been plunged into Lou's eyes. A hammer Lou normally used to break coal was located nearby in the coal shed, covered in blood. This attack was personal.

Andy was immediately suspected, but there was not enough evidence to convict him. There was a witness. A neighbor, Andrew Quinn, had seen Andy with the couple the day of their murder, but there was no evidence tying Andy to the crime. Two trials later and Andy was acquitted of all charges.

A few nights after his acquittal, Andy burst in on his friend Marcus at his barbershop. Andy told Marcus that he had been walking to Frogtown when he spotted George and Lou walking arm in arm. He was certain it was them, as George was singing his favorite song. Lou smiled up at George as the lovers walked together. Andy nearly fainted when the lovers continued their stroll and walked right through him! Trembling as he told his friend the story, Andy broke down in tears. Marcus took control of the situation by giving Andy a drink to steady his nerves. Andy had already been drinking and it was a foggy night. Marcus reasoned that anyone was prone to see things in Andy's situation, especially after the stress of a murder trial.

Did Andy see the ghosts of George and Lou? Was it a guilty conscience making him see them? No more sightings of George and Lou were recorded after that night. But take a stroll down Dayton Street until you strike mud (now the location of Antioch Midwest), and you may hear the words to "My Pretty Quadroon" floating in the air.

To this old world I'll soon say farewell
My heart will find rest in the tomb
But my spirit will fly to the spot
And watch over my pretty quadroon.

VALLANDIGHAM'S GHOST

The Golden Lamb in Lebanon is as old as Ohio itself. When Jonas Seaman came to Ohio from New Jersey to open an establishment for public entertainment, he hung a sign out front with a picture of a golden lamb on it. Many travelers could not read back then, so the sign was a way for them to distinguish his business from others. Eventually, Golden Lamb became the name of the hotel and restaurant.

In the ensuing two hundred years, the Golden Lamb has played host to numerous famous people, including twelve U.S. presidents, Mitt Romney, Barbara Bush, Annie Oakley, Charles Dickens, Harriet Beecher Stowe, Mark Twain, Neil Armstrong and, in recent years, Kesha. There are so many more to name, but one in particular hails from Dayton and haunts the second-floor room that bears his name.

Clement Vallandigham was a political activist and lawyer. His outspoken nature could both help and hurt him. Vallandigham aligned himself with the Peace Democrats, an organization also nicknamed "Copperheads" for their snakelike, poisonous ways. As a staunch Copperhead, he spoke out in sympathy for the Confederacy, an act that got him arrested and "deported" to the South as punishment. He was allowed back when he agreed to certain terms from President Abraham Lincoln. Vallandigham's political career continued while he also practiced law.

As a lawyer, Vallandigham was known for switching between prosecution and defense. He picked sides based on the case and on his chance of winning.

Golden Lamb sign.

Vallandigham had a reputation for doing thorough research and evoking deep feelings with his impassioned arguments. It was this reputation coupled with his defense of Thomas McGehean in a prior criminal case that led McGehean to hire Vallandigham again when McGehean was arrested for the murder of Tom Myers during a barroom brawl.

McGehean and Myers were sworn enemies and when the shot was fired in the bar that evening, McGehean was the first suspect. He immediately hired Vallandigham to defend him, which proved to be the right choice. After spending the day in a field shooting at pieces of fabric from various distances to match the powder burns from the victim's clothing, Vallandigham was ready to show his fellow attorneys working the case what he thought happened that night. Excitedly, he set the loaded gun he used in the field on a table next to the unloaded gun they planned to use for demonstration in court. He ignored his colleagues' warnings to unload the gun or move it away from the unloaded gun before launching into his story. As Vallandigham explained the details of his investigation to his co-counsel, he re-created what he thought happened that night. During the brawl in the bar, someone threw stones at Myers. To defend himself, Myers pulled a gun from the inside pocket of his jacket. It was during this act, Vallandigham claimed, that the gun caught on his jacket and fired, shooting Myers in the stomach. It was simply an accident. In his vigor to tell the story, Vallandigham grabbed the wrong gun from the table and, in performing the same actions as Myers, shot himself the same way. Vallandigham died the following day.

Since his untimely death in 1871, many have sworn they've seen Vallandigham in the second-floor room where he died, known as the Vallandigham Room. He has also been seen hanging out in the Corwin Room on the same floor. People report seeing a man wearing old-fashioned clothes and often wearing a stovepipe hat. When a tourist at the Golden Lamb took a picture of the room, they swore they saw the clear outline of his face in the photo. A housekeeper saw a man fitting Vallandigham's description sitting on a bench in the fourth-floor hallway while she was

HON. C. L. VALLANDIGHAM,

Accidentally shooting himself.

Sketch depicting Vallandigham accidentally killing himself. *Public domain.*

up there cleaning. Another housekeeper heard a heavy sigh and turned around and saw nothing. The sigh is one of the more common experiences with Vallandigham. Perhaps he sighs when he thinks about the way he died. Do ghosts think back to embarrassing moments and heave deep sighs, the way we do?

MORNINGSTAR ROAD

If you park at the horse trailer lot on Morningstar Road you will see an old chimney in the woods across the street. According to legend, this chimney belonged to a house that burned down with children inside.

Back in the 1800s, a man built his family a brick house in a remote part of Morningstar Road. The father of the children belonged to a social club and went to Germantown for a meeting, leaving his wife and their four children in the house. After the mother put the children to bed, she went out back to finish some chores, leaving the windows open so she could hear if her children cried out for her. She was busy with a task when a strong wind from a storm blew a lace curtain into the flame of a kerosene lamp inside, engulfing the front of the house in flames. Engrossed with her chores, she did not see the flames curling up the sides of the house. By the time she noticed the fire, it had already spread to the front door and staircase, cutting off the only path to her children sleeping upstairs.

She braved the flames as a mother would, trying to find another way in to save her children. She beat at the flames with a quilt but only fanned them more. When she knew she couldn't do anything more to get to them, she rushed out to the street, calling for help. Unfortunately, no one was around. When the roof caved in, she sprang into action, running through the woods and screaming for help. In her frantic state, she did not see the thick tree branch in front of her and ran straight into it, breaking her neck instantly. As she died in the woods, her children died in the house. In another version of this story, she ran into the woods in grief after realizing her children died.

The grieving mother still haunts the remains of her former property and the surrounding woods, beckoning to passersby for help. If you roll your car windows down, you can hear screaming, but it is unclear if it's the children who were inside the burning house or their mother, helpless to save her children.

DEATH OF A SENATOR

Arthur Brown was a motivated man. In 1862, as the youngest graduate of Antioch College (now Antioch University), he told his classmates he'd be a senator in ten years. While it took more time than that, he did become senator. Senator Brown's interest in politics did not make him famous, however. It was his womanizing ways. Brown divorced his first wife, Lydia Coon, to marry Isabel Cameron. When Brown left Cameron to be with mistress Anne Bradley, Cameron had Brown and Bradley both arrested for adultery. Bradley had two children with Brown, and although she pushed him to marry, he kept postponing the date.

When Senator Brown traveled to Washington, D.C., to argue a case in front of the Supreme Court, Bradley heard a rumor that he was running around with another woman. Enraged, she traveled to D.C. to confront him. She rented a room at the same hotel and confronted him in his room. While in the room, she saw letters he had been exchanging with another woman, Anne Kiskadden.

Not wanting to continue the argument, Senator Brown turned around and walked away. This only angered Bradley more, and she pulled out a gun and shot him. It took Brown four days to die. Bradley was arrested for her crime but ultimately acquitted, having acquired immense sympathy from the general public. After the drama of the court case died down, Bradley found herself entangled in more drama when she discovered that Brown had excluded her children from her marriage to Mr. Bradley from his will but left money for the children Brown and Bradley had together. This caused resentment among her children, as it was rumored she also favored Brown's children. Years later, two of her sons, Matthew Bradley (a son from her marriage) and Arthur Brown Jr. (a son of Arthur Brown), got into an argument, and Matthew shot and killed Arthur.

Ten years after this drama, a farmer traveling in his carriage noticed a couple walking along Dayton Yellow Springs Road around midnight. He stopped to offer them a ride. As they traveled together in the carriage, the farmer chatted amicably with the couple, but eventually they fell silent as they neared their destination. The farmer thought nothing of it at the time and continued chatting until he came to a stop outside the house they wanted to visit. He was startled to turn around and see nobody in the back seat of his carriage. His passengers had vanished into thin air. Frightened, he drove away in a hurry. He later was able to identify the couple from newspaper pictures as Anne Bradley and Senator Arthur Brown. While attending Antioch College, Brown was known for taking long strolls through Yellow Springs at midnight. Did Senator Brown and Anne Bradley come to Yellow Springs to take a midnight stroll? The farmer insists they did.

5

EERIE EATERIES

AMBER ROSE

When Sigmunt Kseizopolski (pronounced "chez-a-polski") opened his general store and deli, Sig's, in 1910, it was in the heart of Dayton's densely populated Eastern European neighborhood. Once opened, the store quickly became a meeting place of sorts for the Polish community. Meetings, celebrations and evening card games were held at Sig's. Sig, his wife and their six children lived on the second and third floors. During the Great Flood of 1913, the National Guard stayed with the Kseizopolski family in the house.

One of Sig's daughters, Genevieve, especially loved her father's store. While the rest of her siblings got married and moved out, Genevieve, nicknamed Chickee (also spelled Chickie and Chicky), stayed behind with her parents and never married. Chickie was born the same year the store opened, and she happily lived the rest of her days in the house / general store until her death in 1983. Chickee is buried in Calvary Cemetery with her family.

In 1989, Elinor Sluzas bought Sig's and began renovating it into a restaurant serving Eastern European cuisine, including cabbage rolls, potato pancakes, pierogies and sauerkraut. Just before opening, a fire broke out. A portion of the structure had to be rebuilt. Despite the setbacks, Sluzas was still able to open the Amber Rose Restaurant in 1990. Her employees soon

Amber Rose Restaurant, located at 1400 Valley Street.

reported dishes crashing to the floor, music turning on and off by itself, strange laughter and sweet singing. Sluzas later learned the identity of the ghost after having a conversation at a grocery store with Rose Losko, one of Sigmunt Kseizopolski's daughters. Rose revealed that she suspected her sister Chickee to be the ghost and that after her death she came back to the place she loved so much. Sluzas retired in 1998 and sold the restaurant to Joe Castellano, the current owner. He has kept all the recipes the same. Another thing that stayed the same was the ghostly sightings. It didn't take long before the sightings and experiences picked up again.

Many visitors to the Amber Rose Restaurant have experienced seeing someone in the bathroom mirror but when they turn around, nobody is there. Polka music is often heard playing. Employees have seen apparitions and experienced a sense of being watched. Dishes fall off the shelves, items are moved and one night an employee saw a blue ball of light inside the kitchen. A cook reported seeing Chickee walk into the kitchen, lift her ruffled dress and then exit the room. The security camera shows a white orb of light following the path Chickee took at that exact time. Neighbors to Amber Rose have seen a young woman with dark hair wearing a white nightgown walking inside after hours. The sightings take place mostly in the attic, which was once a living space for Chickee. A ghostly man has been reported by a paranormal investigation team to be haunting the basement. Maybe he is there to keep Chickee company. The majority of things experienced by the staff and neighbors seem more like harmless pranks than malice. Perhaps Chickee wants to make sure everyone knows she is still here in the house she loved so much.

ARBY'S MIAMISBURG

This Arby's location boasts more than roast beef sandwiches. Employees feel watched when going into the basement and several have heard the sound of children laughing and have seen mysterious shadows. The hanging plants swing in the dining room when there is no air circulating. In some cases, employees have had their hair pulled and have stepped back into a large object but when they turn around nothing is there. An apparition of a bald man has been spotted in the kitchen staring at the oven when nobody but employees are present.

PIZZA HUT, KETTERING

Employees working after hours at the Pizza Hut on Whipp Road often hear banging on the windows next to the drive thru. Nobody is there when the sounds are investigated. The fountain drink machine dispenses at random times throughout the day when no one is around to operate it. Many believe it may be the ghost of a former employee.

YE OLDE TRAIL TAVERN

If you visit Yellow Springs, take time to stop by Ye Olde Trail Tavern. It was the first home built in the city, which was then known as Forest Village. The tavern was intended to be used as a stagecoach stop on the route between Columbus and Cincinnati. The trees cleared from the land were used to build the tavern.

But this isn't the only reason to visit. Along with its German-inspired cuisine, Ye Olde Trail Tavern offers another attraction: ghosts. A popular version of the story tells of two female ghosts residing in different parts of the house, one upstairs and the other downstairs. They are polar opposites in many ways, connected by marriage as mother and daughter-in-law. Many refer to the pair as the happy ghost and the sad ghost.

The ghost downstairs (the happy ghost) is an older woman, thought to be Mary Hafner. She is seen wearing a blue-and-white-print dress and wearing her blond hair in a bun. Although pleasant, she will make it known if she doesn't like something, especially being mocked. The owner of the tavern wanted to play a prank on her friends, who came looking for ghostly activity. She thought nothing of jumping out to scare them, but when she got to work the next day, all the food in her walk-in fridge had frozen solid. She had no choice but to throw out all the food, The repairman she hired could find nothing wrong and had no explanation for the frozen food. A guest who had openly mocked the hauntings (and called them publicity stunts) witnessed an ashtray split in half before his eyes. He became a believer then and there. The majority of the ghostly activity involves interference with electronics, knocking over furniture and whispers.

In life, Mary Hafner loved her husband and their tavern. On his deathbed, he asked his wife to take care of the place. Although it was a bit overwhelming, she obliged. She remains to this day, taking care of the place she and her husband loved so dearly. Her presence in the tavern is felt mostly in pranks and a pleasant-looking apparition with a friendly smile seen walking from the front to the back.

In stark contrast to the senior Mrs. Hafner is her daughter-in-law, Rebecca Hafner, the upstairs ghost. Mary and Frank Hafner's son William was not a good character. He had a child with a woman named Hattie Birch in 1874 but refused to see the child, Nettie. He also had no trouble deceiving or cheating to get his way.

William wanted to marry Rebecca, but she was in love with someone else and refused to consider William's proposal. When her lover went away to fight in the Civil War, William paid to intercept the letters her soldier sent home to her. After several months of receiving no communication from her lover, Rebecca presumed him to be dead. Devastated, she agreed to marry William. Already unhappy with the arrangement, Rebecca was absolutely distraught when her true love returned from war and she learned the truth of what William did. There was an age difference of about twenty years between William and Rebecca, and many believe she hoped to remarry after

Ye Olde Trail Tavern.

his death. Unfortunately for her, he stipulated in his will that she was never to have another husband. "I request my wife, for reasons of my own, not to remarry," he wrote. Rebecca adhered to the request, never remarrying. In the will, William left the entirety of his estate to Rebecca, with the exception of the paltry sum of ten dollars to his illegitimate daughter, Nettie. Visitors upstairs feel an intense sadness and often see a woman with long, loose, dark hair wearing an ankle-length, dark-colored dress. She can be seen sitting in a corner of the room looking out the window and crying. She has also been spotted in the ladies' room, which is upstairs. Anyone who sees her reports a sad-looking woman in the mirror who disappears quickly.

Interestingly enough, most women do not report any sightings. The majority of witnesses to the ghostly activity are men with ponytails, a population not in short supply in Yellow Springs.

MUDLICK TAVERN, DOWNTOWN DAYTON

Employees of Mudlick Tavern, formerly a bar known as Aquarius, have reported seeing people walk by when nobody is around. Chairs move on their own after hours, when no customers are left in the building and most of the employees have gone home. Employees from Aquarius reported the same occurrences when that bar occupied the space, especially in the dressing room in the basement. The building was erected about 1910, so speculation is that the ghosts in residence may have died in the 1913 flood.

SUNRISE CAFÉ

With vegetarian, vegan and locally sourced options, food practically flies off the shelves at this Yellow Springs eatery. In fact, sometimes it does! Loaves of bread have been known to fly off the shelves on their own. Other items are thrown from countertops and shadowy figures are seen walking past but when employees turn to look nobody is there. The front doorbell rings when nobody has walked in and an old woman has been spotted multiple times seated at a table along the wall on the right. In the blink of an eye, she disappears.

FLORENTINE HOTEL AND RESTAURANT, GERMANTOWN

The second-oldest inn in Ohio was opened in the early 1800s by Phillip Gunckel, founder of Germantown. Guests arrived in stagecoaches, on horseback, in covered wagons and via the traction line. The fireplace on the first floor is the original fireplace used to keep guests warm during their stay. Food was cooked downstairs in a basement fireplace and sent up by dumbwaiter to the first-floor dining room. Visitors to the hotel and restaurant have experienced doors opening and closing by themselves and heavy breathing coming from behind closed doors. Muffled voices can be heard on all levels and loud banging is heard from the pipes in the basement. A poltergeist has been blamed for chandeliers swinging back and forth and objects being moved around. Feelings of being watched and shadows on the wall are common occurrences and an eerie presence on the third floor has been reported from guests who stay the night.

BENNETT'S PUBLICAL FAMILY SPORTS GRILL

Author and blogger Rosella Rowe reported feeling a male presence upstairs the first time she dined at this Miamisburg eatery. She felt he had died in the room upstairs, potentially in a fire. Another time, she reported feeling a female presence in the bathroom. Each time, the waitstaff was not surprised by her experiences, as they have often had their own. Rowe has returned many times and has had an experience each time. Employees and patrons have reported feeling a heavy presence and one customer asked to move tables because the atmosphere at her table made her uncomfortable.

6

SUPERNATURAL STAGES

BLUE JACKET AMPHITHEATER

The Blue Jacket Amphitheater was named for Shawnee chief Blue Jacket. A war chief of the Shawnee people, he was known for defending his land in Ohio. As the story goes, Blue Jacket got his name because he always wore a blue hunting jacket. The Shawnee gave him the name Weyapiersenwah ("Wey-yah-pih-ehr-sehn-weh"), which translates to "Blue Jacket."

Decades after his death, a story emerged that Blue Jacket was actually a white man named Marmaduke Van Swearingen who had been adopted by the Shawnee people. This version of the story was very popular, and a play depicting this version of the story, *Blue Jacket, White Shawnee War Chief*, was performed at the Blue Jacket Amphitheater from 1981 until 2007, when bankruptcy forced the venue to close for good. The amphitheater has since been demolished.

Historical records written by people who personally knew Blue Jacket never mention an alternate identity, and records prove that Van Swearingen and Blue Jacket were different ages. There are records of different life events proving they could not be the same person. Blue Jacket was documented to have already been a war chief by the time Van Swearingen was adopted into the Shawnee Nation. A DNA test in 2000 with samples from known descendants of each man finally proved without a doubt that Van Swearingen and Blue Jacket were not the same person.

The live outdoor performance was a popular attraction. For many in the area, it was their only experience with live theater. Real horses and real guns made the performance come alive and feel authentic to the audience. The stage blended in with the wooded surroundings. Sometimes, members of the audience believed extras for the show were coming out from the woods. However, actors in the woods were not part of the performance and it is believed that the "extras" the audience saw were ghosts of Native Americans showing up to watch the performance. An actor practicing with a drum reported feeling as if a crowd was forming around him. He felt watched, but when he stopped playing the drum and looked around, he no longer felt like anyone was there.

SORG OPERA HOUSE

Known as the "Last of the Robber Barons," Paul Sorg was the second-wealthiest man in Ohio. He trained to be an iron worker before serving in the Civil War. After the war, Sorg paired up with John Auer, a German immigrant who knew tobacco but couldn't keep books. Sorg knew how to keep books but didn't know tobacco. Together, they formed Wilson, Sorg, and Company with other locals in Middletown. Soon after opening, Auer and Sorg sold their shares and opened their own tobacco company. It was a great success and Sorg became Middletown's first multimillionaire. He owned a paper company, tobacco concerns, railroad interests and real estate. He even loaned $6,000 to James Cox so he could buy the *Dayton Daily News*. Sorg also served as a member of Congress and ran for governor twice.

Susan Jennie Sorg (known as Jennie), Paul's wife, was obsessed with theater. Sorg built the Sorg Opera House for her in 1891 to run and operate as she liked. The venue hosted live opera, early forms of motion pictures (such as photo plays), vaudeville performances and the first talkie in Middletown.

In 1935 a fire broke out, resulting in over $10,000 in damages to the opera house, equivalent to roughly $185,298 today. It closed for several months for renovations and reopened in late 1935. More renovations followed in the 1940s, and the upper balcony was closed off to improve sound quality. Sorg operated again until the 1970s, then closed, then reopened later. It operated until 2010, when a water-main break forced it to close again. Sorg Opera House reopened again in 2012 and then underwent major repairs and renovations, reopening to the public in 2017.

Ghost of Paul Sorg

When he died in 1902, Paul Sorg's funeral was held in the Sorg Opera House after a private service in the morning. His body lay in state for four hours so the residents of Middletown could pay their respects. Sorg still hangs around the theater watching the performances from his favorite seat, the middle seat in the first row on the first balcony, wearing full evening attire. He has been seen by janitors, actors, caretakers and stagehands. He's easily identified by his portrait in the lobby. If approached, his spirit disappears.

Lady in the Red Dress

Another spirit hanging around the Sorg Opera House is a woman in a red dress. She was an actress at Sorg who disappeared one night, never to be seen again. Her red dress was the only thing remaining in her dressing room. Her spirit has been spotted wearing the dress while applying makeup in her dressing room and she can be heard singing throughout the theater. She disappears if she realizes she has been seen. The scent of sweet-smelling perfume lingers long after she disappears.

Catwalk Ghost

Sounds of footsteps can be heard on the catwalks. It is believed that a stagehand fell off the catwalk and died and his spirit remains behind. He can be heard running back and forth as if trying to find a way down.

Peanut Gallery

During the early years of Sorg Opera House, African Americans could only attend the theater using a separate entrance to the upper balcony. Only peanuts were served on the upper balcony. Although peanuts are no longer served at Sorg Opera House, staff and theater patrons still find them on the floor.

TOWN HALL THEATER

Town Hall Theater in Washington Township was opened in 1908 as a gathering place for meetings, graduations and other activities. The building housed government offices until 1985. In 1989, township officials decided to turn the building into a performing arts center.

Town Hall Theater presents about eight to ten plays for young audiences each season. It is owned by the Washington Township Recreation Center, which sponsors performing arts summer camps at the theater. Each year the theater performs for over twenty thousand audience members and uses over four hundred community volunteers.

The ghost of Washington Township's Town Hall Theater is described as a tall man resembling Abraham Lincoln. He is often seen in the upstairs bedroom and peering out the window. Although this ghost is said to physically resemble former president Lincoln, his behavior does not. This ghost does not like any plays with profanity or anything he considers lewd. Lincoln was known for enjoying a good risqué joke. He will make it known if he does not like something performed on stage by putting out the theater's pilot light and acting up during the performance. He is also said to intensely dislike women and will bother them the most. The basement often has cold spots and is considered to be darker than a normal basement. The lights for the stage will go on and off by themselves.

MIAMISBURG PLAZA THEATER

This theater was opened in 1916 and was once seen as the jewel of the community and brought people in for plays and eventually movies. Although there are supposed to be many ghosts in the theater, the one that stands out to witnesses is the ghost of the homeless man in the basement. In the mid-1960s, the man stayed in the basement in exchange for doing odd jobs around the theater. After about a year, he was suddenly found dead in the basement. In the room where he died, a stool sits in the exact spot where he died. If anyone moves the stool, it will move itself back to the spot.

MEMORIAL HALL

Memorial Hall is located at 125 East First Street and is home to the Dayton Philharmonic. It was added to the National Register of Historic Places in July 1988. A janitor named Drake fell into the orchestra pit and died. His ghost flushes toilets and plays with the lights and his footsteps can be heard walking across the catwalk. Drake likes to hang out in sections of the theater that are less trafficked, often surprising people who walk into those rooms with the sight of his apparition. The sounds of whispered conversations can be heard in the Cabaret Room.

VICTORIA THEATER

Originally opened in 1866 as the Turner Opera House, the Victoria Theater went through a long list of names before being named Victoria Theater, for the late queen of England after her death in 1901. The venue was renamed Victory Theater during World War I to be patriotic and the name continued for a few decades until being changed to Victoria Theater for the last time. Throughout its 150-plus years, Victoria Theater has witnessed much of Dayton's history, including some stories of its own.

Lucille

One such story is that of Lucille, a lovely young theater patron attacked in her theater box at stage right (or house left, meaning the box to the left if you are facing the stage). Although she had been accompanied by an escort to the theater that night, her escort was lured away, leaving her vulnerable. A man attacked Lucille, attempting to sexually assault and then murder her. Luckily for her, patrons nearby heard her screams and came running to her aid, preventing her attacker from removing her clothing. Although Lucille survived this attack and lived a long life after moving out of Dayton, the attack left an indelible impression on the theater box. Only men with a vicious temperament have reported any experiences. These men feel chills, shoves, major temperature changes and, in some cases, violent attacks. Perhaps ladies who wish to know if their man is a good guy can take him for a show in the house left box at the theater.

Victoria Theater, named for the late Queen Victoria.

Suicidal Ghost

Another ghost in attendance is the suicidal ghost. A man reportedly wedged a large knife in a seat in the left section of the theater in the twentieth row. He then impaled himself on the knife, leaving a large mess to be cleaned. His blood ran down the floor, pooling into the orchestra pit. The man's ghostly visage could be seen on the curtains leading backstage until eventually they were replaced with doors and the sightings stopped. The story has few other details and it's been claimed to have occurred anywhere from the 1880s to the 1950s.

Vickie

One cannot mention the ghosts of Victoria Theater without mentioning Vickie (also spelled Vicky) herself. Her nickname stems from the name of the theater, as any tie to a specific actress has been lost over time. Vickie was a traveling actress performing in the Victoria Theater in the early 1900s.

During a costume change between scenes, Vickie ran up the stairs to change into a black taffeta dress. As she descended the stairs in the dress, she stopped and turned around, passing a male costar on the steps. "I forgot my fan," she said to him as she passed. She was last seen walking into her dressing room and shutting the door behind her. When she missed her stage cue in the next scene, the frustrated stage manager burst into her dressing room, only to find it empty. A search of the room revealed that the black taffeta dress and the matching black fan were missing. There was no sign of Vickie.

The mystery of where Vickie went still has not been solved. There were only two ways Vickie could have left the theater from her dressing room that night. One way would have been back down the same staircase where her costar had last seen her. If she had used that staircase, the security guard on duty would have seen her leave. The only other possible way out was a third-story window that had not been opened that night. If Vickie had opened and left through the window, there would have been no ladder or other prop with which she could have climbed down outside.

The primary theory as to what happened to Vickie is that she was murdered in her dressing room and her body hidden until it could be safely removed from the theater unseen. Another theory was that Vickie herself was responsible for her disappearance, hiding in the theater until everyone left, then running off with a lover.

Since her disappearance, Vickie's dressing room has been used less and less frequently over the years. When actors used the dressing room, they saw her face in the mirror, only to whirl around and see nobody behind them. Actors climbing up and down the staircase would feel the sensation of someone brushing against them. They would also get whiffs of Vickie's favorite rose-scented perfume and hear the rustling of her taffeta dress as if she was walking in the dressing room beside them. They also had difficulty keeping the door to her dressing room closed. The light taps of a woman's high-heeled shoes can be heard crossing the stage. Vickie loves to play with the elevator, often pressing buttons and calling the elevator to each floor. She likes to turn off the bathroom light when it's being cleaned and has appeared as a headless apparition wearing a black dress a few times.

During renovations to the theater, Vickie made her displeasure known by moving the construction workers' tools when they'd leave for breaks.

In the 1990s, WDTN Channel 2 went to Victoria Theater to tape a Halloween segment. The anchor heard a rustling sound. When the sound recording was later checked to see if the noise was picked up, it was. It was described as the sound of taffeta rustling, as if someone was wearing a dress of that material and walking. Maybe Vickie stuck around after all, perhaps for an interview or one last curtain call.

There is a theory that Vickie has been mixed up with the disappearance of Lillian Graham, an actress who disappeared the night before a performance in 1911 from a Victoria Theater in New York City. Graham, along with her costar and roommate, Ethel Conrad, was awaiting trial for the attempted murder of W.E.D. Stokes, a man with whom they'd both been having an affair. Graham disappeared for a few days, then reappeared with a story that she had been kidnapped. The similarities of an actress disappearing from a theater of the same name and time frame have led some to believe that Lillian Graham is "Vickie."

In 1970, nine teenagers stayed overnight in the theater to hunt for ghosts. The teenagers, who were students from Northridge High School, brought with them tape recorders, two-way radios and snacks. One student, who was part of a radio program called *In Search of the Unknown*, had the idea while interviewing an employee of Victoria Theater (then called Victory Theater). Among the stories the employee shared was that of Vickie, the ghost of the actress who supposedly disappeared. Using blueprints of the original layout of the theater, the group, accompanied by two teachers from their school, knocked out walls looking for her remains. Unfortunately, all they found were old posters and theater memorabilia. By the end of the night, all the group had for their search were a few unexplained whispers and an image someone saw in a chair.

7
ENDURING ENTITIES

DAYTON DAILY NEWS BUILDING, FOURTH AND LUDLOW

Shortly after James M. Cox bought the *Dayton Evening News* in 1898, he changed the name to *Dayton Daily News*. After getting the paper running successfully, Cox turned his attention to politics and ran for governor of Ohio, then for president with running mate Franklin D. Roosevelt. Although he did not win the election, Cox remained active in politics for decades. He moved to Van Buren Township (now known as Kettering), where he built a mansion near both Charles Kettering and Edward Deeds. James M. Cox died in 1957.

A year after his death, a new janitor was hired at the *Dayton Daily News* building and was sent upstairs to clean. He came back downstairs almost immediately and told his boss he had encountered a man in a smoking jacket who identified himself as James Cox. The mysterious man then asked to be left alone. The man told him it was ok to not clean the study and then disappeared. The janitor was able to verify the identity of the ghost by viewing a portrait of James Cox. The building is not used by the newspaper anymore but while it was, employees reported strange noises and the elevator operating on its own, opening and closing on random floors. The apparition of James Cox has also been spotted working in the third-floor library.

NORMANDY CHURCH

Normandy Church in Centerville was once a private mansion built in the early 1900s. It was part of the 780-acre Normandy Farm estate built by Richard Grant Sr., who made his money in sales with NCR, Delco Light and General Motors. The house was constructed between 1927 and 1930, costing nearly $1 million. There are eleven sculptured marble fireplaces, stained-glass window plaques, huge entrance gates and hand-carved wood paneling. When Grant Sr. died in 1957, his estate was divided into Normandy Church, Grant Park, Normandy Elementary, Grant Life Center and residential housing. When the house was converted into a church, the church added a chapel and music room. Normandy United Methodist Church is still active and so is the ghost of a previous resident, perhaps Mrs. Grant. The nighttime cleaning staff reports hearing mysterious noises as they clean and they have smelled women's perfume. During these incidents, no one else is in the building. According to legend, one of the servants tried to commit suicide by jumping from the top of the spiral staircase. Although she survived her fall, her spirit remains in the house, which is still desolate.

DAYTON VETERAN MEDICAL CENTER

Dayton Veteran Medical Center was established by congressional legislation signed by President Lincoln in 1865. Dayton received the first Civil War veteran in 1867. Today, it's a modern healthcare facility that strives to continue Lincoln's promise "to care for him who shall have borne the battle, and for his widow, and his orphan."

Although modernized, the building has several original occupants roaming the hallways.

Freedom House

The Freedom House is host to a party from the 1870s still going on to this day. Music can be heard at random times throughout the day and night. The partygoers have been seen wearing post–Civil War era clothing and having a great time.

The third floor of the Freedom House has the most ghostly activity. The sounds of crying can be heard when nobody is around. Footsteps tread where nobody else walks. Overall, a presence can be felt by staff members. A gray mist was seen moving down the hallway and coming down the stairs from the third floor. When the employee who saw it reacted, her coworker turned around and saw it too.

Liberty House

A spirit believed to be Brigadier General Marsena Patrick haunts Liberty House. Just before the start of the Battle of Petersburg in June 1864, General Patrick felt ill and laid down under a tree to rest. He passed out immediately and was treated by doctors with electrical shocks, mercury pills and other horrendous treatments common at the time. It's possible that he experienced a heart attack, as he reported pain in his left arm earlier that day. By September, his entire left side was paralyzed and he was no longer able to be in the service. He was granted a disability pension. As a result of his medical treatment, he experienced seizures. In those days, seizures were considered akin to mental illness and thus shameful and to be hidden at all costs. Patrick locked himself away any time he felt a seizure coming on. His presence can be felt in the small room where he hid away. Many visitors feel despair and sadness in the house. Recording equipment and cameras often do not work inside Liberty House but as soon as they are taken out of the building, they work again just fine.

Patient Library

People working in the Patient Library report feeling a sense of being watched, as if someone is looking over their shoulder. A ghostly woman can be seen looking out the upper windows and a handprint will be found on the window after it's been cleaned. A ghostly librarian shushes loud visitors.

MASONIC TEMPLE

The Dayton Masonic Temple, now known as the Dayton Masonic Center, sits atop a hill next to the Dayton Art Institute. This building took nearly three years to complete by 450 workers who were mostly Masonic brethren. The building is now a contributing property in the Steele's Hill–Grafton Hill Historic District, which was added to the National Register of Historic Places in 1986. Amid the historic architecture of the building resides a ghost named George. George is a former Mason who attended in 1962 and decided to stick around in the afterlife in the place he loved. George likes to roam the entire building while other ghosts like to stay in specific rooms.

The lounge of the Masonic Center is another story. While George is a warm and welcoming presence to all who come to the center, the lounge is an uncomfortable place to be for women. They have reported feeling uncomfortable as if they have entered somewhere they aren't supposed to be. The lounge, which used to be for gentlemen only, has a heavy, unwelcoming atmosphere. Most women do not like to stay in the room longer than they have to.

Other ghostly presences include an apparition of an older member who liked to doze in a lounge chair while watching TV. He was removed from that chair and taken to the hospital when he had the stroke that killed him. After death, he returned to his chair in the place he loved to watch TV and doze again. Sounds of high-heeled shoes clack on the floor when nobody is around. The water fountain will turn on for a few seconds and then turn off, as if someone has taken a drink. Elevators operate on their own, going to various floors and opening as if someone is riding in them. Doors open and close by themselves. The Commandery Asylum, a meeting room on the third floor, is haunted by a spirit who roams the balcony.

EDEN HALL

Not to be confused with Cincinnati's Eden Park, which is also haunted, Eden Hall is one of Xenia's most historic buildings. It was built in 1840 by Abram Hivling. Abram and his family lived in the house until 1881, when he sold it to his niece and her husband, who gave the house to their daughter Mary and her husband, Coates Kinney. Coates Kinney was a lawyer, journalist and government paymaster during the Civil War. He owned the *Xenia Torchlight* and was well known in the literary world. Together, Coates and Mary had three daughters. One of the daughters did not get along well with the family and so lived on the third floor by herself. She had the reputation of being a difficult person to like. She often dressed oddly to embarrass her family. Her son's two daughters inherited the house.

The house stands three stories tall, each level thirteen feet high. The house was named Eden Hall by Mrs. Kinney, a reference to returning "back to Eden" after she had been away for a while traveling. The interior is divided into forty-two rooms (ten of which are in the basement), and there are over 750 paintings. The home has passed through many hands and opened as a bed-and-breakfast in the early 2000s. The building is now a private residence but still has many guests coming through, although they are not the kind to check in and out. The Kinney family is said to have never truly left the place. They remain behind along with the cranky ghost of a woman on the third floor, presumed to be the daughter who in life did not get along well with the family. She's been known to knock things over, slam doors and play music when she is upset in order to make her presence known.

Ghostly footprints have appeared in the dust on the third floor, small like children's feet. Mysterious lights are seen in the building and music plays when no one is around. When people are in the house, they often feel as if someone is walking past them despite the place being empty. Doors open and close by themselves and disembodied voices commonly wake up anyone sleeping in the house. The party doesn't stop for the Kinney family, no matter how many years have passed. Sounds of talking, laughing and party music can be heard at night when the house is still.

THE OLD COURTHOUSE

On the northwest corner of Third and Main Streets sits the old Montgomery County Courthouse. It was built in 1847, modeled after the Temple of Hephaestus in Athens. The Greek Revival courthouse is made of limestone and includes a high-ceiling vestibule, a rotunda and an elliptical courtroom.

Dayton resident Horace Pease suggested the idea, showing Montgomery County commissioners a book of sketches of the Acropolis in Athens. The commissioners were impressed and hired architect Howard Daniels of New

York to draw the plans. The courthouse was added to the National Register of Historic Places as of January 1970.

When the courthouse was finished, the first case heard in the old courthouse was a divorce. Later, as the Civil War divided Dayton, the heavy iron doors and windows protected the building from angry mobs. Until a jail could be built, the courthouse also held prisoners.

Hangings were a crowd attraction. During its time as an active courthouse, many hangings were performed. This included the hanging of Francis Dick, who had to be hanged twice for his crime. Dick had been convicted of killing his wife's mother and brother, with money as the motive. While waiting for execution, Dick eventually confessed to the crime and to other violent acts, including another murder before he came to Dayton from Troy. During the hanging, the rope used to make the noose broke and Dick fell through and hit the ground. Although he landed sitting upright, he was knocked unconscious. The officials had to drag the unconscious man back to the top of the scaffolding and struggle to put his limp head through the noose and position him over the trapdoor. This spectacle was too much for many spectators, leading to a lot of crying, gasping and fainting from the crowd. This day was remembered for a long time as "the day the rope broke."

Another prisoner who made an impression on the crowd was John Dobbins. Dobbins was convicted of robbing and killing George Lindemuth after seeing him flashing a wad of cash at a bar. Dobbins followed Lindemuth then robbed and killed him. While on death row, Dobbins attempted to take his own life, but on the day of execution he walked to the platform appearing indifferent to his fate. He danced a hoedown on his way to the scaffold before being restrained by the sheriff. While standing on the trapdoor, he started to dance again. One account of the day has Dobbins grabbing a bucket and turning it over and banging on it like a drum.

With the history of turmoil and hangings, it's not surprising to hear that the old courthouse is haunted. Footsteps are often heard climbing the stairs in the judge's chambers and soft moaning sounds can be heard throughout the building. The criminals hanged in the court are said to still be attached to the land. Some visitors experience a spooky, dreadful atmosphere at the old courthouse. Many feel frightened but cannot explain why. Perhaps the ghosts of the condemned are still there, waiting for another day in court.

8
PHANTOM PHENOMENA

As the winter storm raged outside, the warmth of the inn lulled truck drivers into a relaxed and sleepy state. When truck driver Roy Fitzwater burst into the inn, bringing along with him the cold air from outside, it startled the truckers into full alert. Visibly shaken and pale as a ghost, the normally calm and composed Roy barely said a word, stating only that he was not ill but that he had earlier experienced an unnerving situation on the road. As he ate a sandwich and drank some coffee, the others tried to coax the story out of him. Despite prodding from other truckers, Roy would not share his story that night.

Highway patrol corporal William Harrell watched the scene unfold with interest. Having met Fitzwater before, Harrell knew he was not the type of man to give in to fits of hysteria. The other truckers suggested that Fitzwater stay in the back building, a concrete block structure designed to be used as a dormitory for truckers. Corporal Harrell asked Fitzwater one more time what he saw that evening. Fitzwater simply stated that he'd rather not talk about it because the others would just laugh at him, but that what he experienced was horrible. With one last sip of his coffee, Roy Fitzwater left the inn and headed for St. Louis, leaving Corporal Harrell and the others perplexed at his unusual behavior.

Just a week later, another driver came in visibly shaken and drained of his color. When he sat to drink his coffee, he trembled so much that it spilled on him. The other men knew this man as well and questioned him about his experience. One man asked him if he had recently come into a large amount of cash and was nervous because of that. The man refused to answer any questions and replied that nobody would believe him anyway.

Another week went by, and a third man came to the inn under the same circumstances. Again, Corporal Harrell was present and under the same questioning, this man also declared that something horrible had occurred and that he was not willing to share his story. A few days later, a fourth man came by. Sure enough, he was shaken, pale and steadfastly silent. After a few sips of his coffee, he was gone like the others.

Harrell noticed a pattern with these men. They all had normally composed and calm demeanors, they all thought nobody would believe them and they had all come from the east and left heading west. From this, he deduced the four men must have seen something in the vicinity of the Englewood Dam. The road by the dam was narrow and difficult to navigate even on the best of days. Add an icy layer to the road, and it was downright treacherous. But these were seasoned drivers, Harrell thought to himself. They've driven this route before, and surely there must be plenty of other stretches of road on their routes similar or worse. These men must have seen something distinctly terrible. The next man will tell me, Harrell thought, even if I have to arrest him. If I can't get him to tell me, a judge will.

Corporal Harrell didn't have to wait long. The next time Fitzwater came in, he again looked terrified. This time, Harrell didn't give him a choice to keep it to himself. When Harrell told him about the other three truckers, Fitzwater relented and told his tale. This is the story he told, as quoted in the manuscript "Tales and Sketches of the Great Miami Valley":

I see now that I was wrong not to tell you the first time I was here about a month ago. But since three other men have apparently seen the very same horrible thing I have seen twice while crossing Englewood Dam. I now feel free to tell the whole thing to you. But the reason I didn't tell you before was that I could hardly believe myself that I had actually seen it. It is something so horribly frightening that even now I fear you might not believe it and laugh at me. As you know, we drivers of these great interstate vans are forbidden to take while on duty any intoxicating liquor, not even a small glass of the mildest beer. So I knew that I could not be intoxicated. But what I saw and what those other drivers must have seen too is so incredible and so unreal that I had the feeling I must be losing my mind, that I was having hallucinations. I just dread to talk about it because I felt those fellows at the inn would not believe it and would only laugh at me, and I could hardly blame them if they would.

Now it seems that this thing, whatever or whoever it is, molests only us truck drivers. And it seems to occur only on dark, stormy, and icy nights such as tonight and on my trip through here a month ago. Just as I get to about the middle of the dam, I see a car turn in at the west end and come straight toward me with bright blinding lights, just as if he intended to plunge right into me. I push on my breaks [sic] and try to swerve, knowing that I must use the utmost care lest I go through the barricade and down the side of the dam. But when that car gets to about 200 feet, it turns to the right, the lights go out, but inside the car appears a blue-green light of the most unearthly kind, revealing skull and skeleton at the wheel. You can see the bones all lighted [sic] up with this peculiar uncanny light. I just can't tell you what a shock this gives a man, and it is just about too horrible to describe. It just about takes the life out of you; and it is no wonder that a man thinks he is losing his mind when he sees it. Now I know if three other drivers besides myself have seen this, I am perfectly normal and am not going insane.

After Fitzwater admitted his story, others came forward. As they shared their stories, they learned that all of the incidents happened on stormy nights and that the phantom driver favored the narrow stretches of road near Englewood Dam and Taylorsville Dam along old Highway 40. The phantom would approach a truck from the opposite direction, dim its lights, then put them out completely around 150 to 200 feet from the truck. After a moment of complete darkness, a light would come on within the approaching car to reveal a skeleton bathed in an ethereal blue-green light. The sight is described by many truckers as "horrible looking."

The drivers had enough. They organized a plan to catch this phantom skeleton during one of his "hauntings," but he narrowly escaped, scraping his car against one of the three trucks attempting to trap him. As this story gained momentum, more stories came to light, telling a tale of a glowing skeleton but some said it was a man in a skeleton suit with the bones outlined in luminous paint.

Apparently Highway 40 alone couldn't contain the phantom, as sightings started on Route 7 in Steubenville near the border of Ohio and West Virginia. A truck driver encountered an automobile veering toward him in the same manner, turning the lights out as it got closer to him. This time, however, the phantom got out of the car and did a dance until the trucker drove away.

The drop-off on either side of Highway 40 is eighty feet, making the taunting from the phantom much scarier for truck drivers.

Later, Clark County sheriff J. Arthur Shuman received a letter postmarked Springfield, Ohio, proposing a midnight race with the sheriff, as long as there would be no roadblocks. "The game must be a chase, not a block," the phantom wrote, "The truck drivers are not my equal. I am going to give you a chance to catch me." He then shared that he installed radar, sonar and other equipment of which he doesn't know the name. He also said he intended to equip the vehicle with a TV screen that could spot patrol cars from 3 miles away and that his car could travel up to 125 miles an hour.

"Challenge me in the full of the moon," he wrote. "May your men be equal to the task and live. I am considered to some to be the world's greatest phantom in modern history." The letter was signed with a drawing of a face cut off above the eyes with seven horns protruding from it. Sheriff Shuman had no comment on the letter. Although 150 people showed up to see the race, the phantom did not appear.

Sightings of the phantom began happening more frequently. Occurrences included the following:

DAYTON GHOSTS & LEGENDS

St. Mary's: Two brothers reported seeing the phantom's car filled up with smoke.

Zanesville: Warnings were written in the dust on the side of trucks.

Hillcrest: Standing on the running board while terrorizing drivers, the phantom had also installed speakers playing moans and shrieks.

Lisbon: A phone call was made warning of the phantom's appearance on Route 7 that night.

Wellsville–West Point area: A car making wailing sounds terrorized drivers.

Williamsport: The phantom caused a car accident when a female accomplice to the phantom beckoned to another driver from the running board of her car. Distracted, the driver swerved into a ditch and damaged the fender of his car.

Springfield: A card postmarked Richmond, Indiana, sent to owners of a restaurant claimed the phantom had "moonar." "I am building an extra super phantom car. One of the new gadgets will be moonar. I can have the full of the moon any night I need it. That will confuse the sheriff."

The car accident was the last time the phantom was seen in person and the postcard was the last communication. The phantom of Route 40 at Englewood Dam disappeared with a cloud of blue-green smoke and the sound of wailing dissipating in the distance.

9

MYSTERIOUS MATTERS

ALLIE SIMMS

A young girl in Xenia by the name of Allie Simms was discovered to have the most unusual condition. Allie, the three-year-old daughter of Charles Simms Jr., was described as a small girl with snappy eyes and an uncontrollable temper.

When she was born in Kentucky in 1900, the word *Allie* was visible on her tongue, saving her parents the trouble of figuring out a name for her. The word was so visible and clear that it caused a stir among the doctors in the hospital, who all came to see it. At the age of three, Allie's tongue featured the clear imprint of the number 76 (some papers reported the number as 67). The numbers are sometimes red but usually white.

Once every four weeks, usually on the twenty-ninth of each month, Allie's body would become covered with letters of the alphabet and Bible verses. The writing was legible and about the size of newspaper letters. The skin on her entire body looked like a newspaper with raised letters. The newspapers reporting the situation at the time theorized that the impressions on her skin must have come through from the nervous system of her mother during pregnancy. The letters on Allie's skin were only visible once a month but the numbers on the tongue were visible every day.

Allie's mother died before Allie turned three and her father had sent her to a children's home in Cincinnati. He later took her out because Allie's bad temper would have led to too many punishments from the managers of the home. He brought her to Xenia to be cared for by a woman named Emily Lawrence.

Although Charles Simms did not seem to profit from his daughter's condition, not everyone believed the story of little Allie Simms. The *Democrat and Chronicle* newspaper of Rochester, New York, ran an article speculating about what the little girl did in February, when there is no twenty-ninth for the letters to appear. "The paternal Simms has omitted to state how Allie manages in ordinary Februaries—whether she goes to press early or omits publication altogether"

CARVED IN WHETSTONE

This story appeared in the *Tucson (AZ) Daily Citizen* in September 1904. This is a paraphrased version of the events.

On Easter Day 1900, local real estate dealer W.H. Starry was at his home on 830 South Main Street, sharpening his knife while sitting next to his window. He noticed two boys playing outside and his attention was drawn to their antics. He watched them for a few minutes and then turned his focus back to the whetstone he was using to sharpen the knife. He

The Transfiguration, by Italian Renaissance artist Raphael. Copies of this painting were commonly hung in Victorian homes. *Public domain.*

remembered noticing that it was completely white. The boys outside caught his attention again and he watched, engrossed with their shenanigans. When he turned his attention back to the whetstone in front of him, he was startled by what he saw. In the whetstone, he saw the face of Christ. The particular image was Christ's face as depicted by Italian Renaissance painter Raphael. The painting, called *The Transfiguration*, was a popular portrayal of Christ and commonly hung in Victorian homes. Starry called his neighbors to his home to verify that he saw what he thought he was seeing. It did not take long for word to spread and people came from all corners to see the face in the whetstone. Many thought this was a sign and the religious made predictions.

Starry decided to donate the whetstone to the Dayton Public Library Museum. Once the piece was sealed in a box away from human hands, it is said the color of the face's lips became more defined, the mouth looked more open and the teeth were more noticeable. When he made the donation, Starry appeared before a notary and swore an oath that he did not create or falsify the appearance on the whetstone.

DEAD AND GONE

It was a typical morning at the Reed family home in August 1891 when the oldest son, twenty-five-year-old Charles J. Reed, walked into the house. The family house in Xenia was not very large, containing two bedrooms, the dining room / kitchen area and one sitting room. The family was gathered around the table eating breakfast when Charles entered. He had walked just a few steps past the table when he suddenly collapsed. He fell to the floor in a heap and never woke up.

Immediately, the father sent a boy to fetch a doctor while the remaining family members carried Charles's body into the bedroom and laid him on the bed. Efforts to resuscitate him failed and he was positioned and covered with a sheet until the doctor could arrive.

The doctor walked into the home within twenty minutes of the collapse. He noticed that the door to the bedroom was closed and the entire family was sitting in the room outside it. When he noticed the arrival of the doctor, the father jumped up to open the bedroom door for him. The doctor walked into the bedroom with the grieving members of Charles's family (mother, father, two sisters) close behind. He noticed the rigid outlines of the body under the sheet and a cloth over the face. Through the cloth, the doctor could see facial features and the profile of Charles's face.

When the doctor approached and lifted the cloth from the corpse's face, he was stunned to see nothing under the cloth. He quickly pulled the sheet away from the body and saw only empty space. Despite having seen the outline of a body through the cloth, there was nothing on the bed. Stunned, the family members and doctor simply looked from one another to the bed, speechless. It took a moment for the three ladies present to react, swooning onto the floor. While the doctor attended to the ladies, the father stood in a dumbfounded state, muttering incoherently and staring unseeing into the distance.

Once the ladies were brought back to consciousness, the doctor walked to the only window in the room and studied it. The window was locked from the inside and had clearly not been opened for a while. Since there was no body, no coroner's inquest was held. An investigation into the disappearance was made but no answers have ever been found. Charles J. Reed was dead and gone.

JAMES MURPHY

On January 31, 1875, Barlow Hall, located at the corner of Pearl and Fifth Streets, hosted a wedding for August Scheckelhoff and Agnes Neehaber. Colonel William Dawson, who worked with the groom, volunteered to be the master of ceremonies. When he turned away James Murphy, a well-known hooligan, and his associates, they threatened him. Later, they returned and attacked him. In the scuffle, Colonel Dawson was stabbed. He bled to death before help arrived.

Police followed evidence to James Murphy and arrested him. Public outrage was so intense that Murphy required protection from a lynch mob. He was convicted and sentenced to hang for his crime. Before his hanging, Murphy confided to Sheriff Tom Hellriggle that he knew he was destined to die even before his conviction was read.

When Sheriff Hellriggle asked Murphy how he could know that, Murphy reminded him of an incident in the jail during the trial. Between midnight and 1:00 a.m. one night, everyone was jolted awake by the unearthly howl of a woman. Her piercing wail of anguish terrified everyone in the building, as there was no woman present. It reminded them of the Irish legend of a banshee wailing outside the window. Murphy said he knew it was the spirit of his late mother, crying for her son and his fate. Murphy found religion in his last days and confessed his sins. When he was ready to go, he commented that he may be hanged twice over.

Sheriff Henry Sherrard (misidentified in Dayton papers as Gerard) of Putnam County was brought in as an expert to help with the hanging, as he had participated in hangings before. Although many assume a hanging involves simply grabbing a rope and making a noose, there are other important things to consider. There are four main types of hanging: standard drop, sudden suspension, short drop and long drop. The method used for Murphy was a long drop, which requires the prisoner to be weighed prior to execution. From the prisoner's weight, calculations are then made regarding the length and strength of the rope and the drop length after the trapdoor is open. The length of time for the prisoner to reach the bottom of the drop should be between one-half and three-fourths of a second. If one of those measurements is off, the drop could cause the rope to break or the prisoner to strangle, or the weight of the drop could cause decapitation. Ropes that are too new may be too elastic to snap enough to break the prisoner's neck. Ropes that are too old may be too weak to hold the weight. The rope intended for use on Murphy had been stretched for twenty-four hours suspending a bucket of water. To Sheriff Sherrard, the rope was strong and ready to hold Murphy's weight. To others viewing the rope, it looked weakened.

Murphy did not fight his fate as he walked to the gallows. He made a speech warning young men to straighten up their lives and get on the right track or this would be their fate as well. When the trapdoor below his feet opened, the three-and-a-half-foot drop length created too much stress on the rope, which snapped, plummeting Murphy to the ground below.

The shocked silence of the crowd coupled with the black hood over his head made Murphy think for a moment that he was dead. As the spectators started to react to what happened in front of them, the reality slowly dawned on Murphy that he was still alive and had to do it again. Panic set in as he was helped up. His heart pounded in his chest. Another rope was secured and Murphy was escorted back into position. It was seven minutes between the first and second hanging and it took seventeen minutes for him to die with the second rope.

Did Murphy's late mother visit the jail cell before his conviction and cry for her son? Did she also warn him he'd be hanged twice for his crime? We will never know for sure.

THE WOMAN IN BLACK

In 1864, residents of Chestnut Street in Dayton were plagued by a woman in black flitting across their yards. The woman in black didn't speak; she simply floated back and forth through yards going through the fences until she settled on a house. Whichever house she settled on would soon experience a death in the family. Groups gathered to follow the ethereal woman, but she'd vanish before their eyes. This pattern was repeated until one night when she disappeared and didn't come back.

Six years later, there was another sighting of the woman in black. A man (his name not given in the source) walking along Chestnut Street near Jefferson noticed a friend of his standing outside her house. They exchanged greetings as he walked past and he noticed a woman standing behind her, wearing all black. He thought it odd that his friend did not introduce them. Then the memory of the woman in black flashed in his mind. He whirled around to look and saw her gliding along behind him without making a sound. She stopped when he stopped. He continued along and she did too. They repeated this pattern of stopping and starting until he decided to turn around and charge at her. When he did, she vanished instantly. Nervous, he decided to walk back down Chestnut to see if he could find her again. He passed his friend's house and she was inside, but the lady in black was right where he saw her the first time.

Again, she followed him down the street in the same manner. Every time he halted his pace, she did as well. He examined every streetlight and shadow to see if there was any way that what he saw could have been an illusion, but saw no conditions that could have caused it. Shaken, he made his way home and told nobody of this incident until a few days later when he heard the news of a death in the house where the woman in black stood that night.

BELLBROOK ANGELS

An article in the *Bellbrook Moon* on March 16, 1904, tells of a sighting of angels in the sky on August 19, 1841. The witness was sitting on their porch viewing an unusual band of light in the sky when they noticed neighbors looking in the other direction, excited at what they saw. They turned and saw what they described as angel forms lined up in a procession, marching in full view in the sky. The angels marched in line two by two, a parade of human forms in flowing robes. They appeared to be covered in some type of gauzy material. A group of ten to fifteen pairs would disappear from view and another group would take its place. The forms were so lifelike that the movement of the arms and legs could be distinguished in the distance. The neighbors were very excited, and several families brought out their sick and bedridden relatives to witness the spectacle above. The vision lasted for ten minutes. This event took place around 10:00 p.m. Four hours later, residents were startled to see a meteor shower, which to them looked like stars falling from the sky. Neighbors were knocking at one another's doors to wake them to see the sight. Many were afraid, thinking with the spectacle of angels just hours before that this was the end of times, Judgment Day. The stars fell fast like a blanket of snow and had little to no heat on reaching the earth. In the morning light, the few remaining meteors in the sky were difficult to see and there were no traces left on the ground.

J.W.S. PAUL'S SPELL BOOK

J.W.S. Paul practiced a sect of Christianity often found in Germany. It was partially explained by the Paternoster Theory, which centers on the Tenet Square and is claimed to have been created by early Christians. The Tenet Square, which involves a palindrome illustration of the words *sator, arepo, tenet, opera* and *rotas*, along with a multitude of spells, has been credited with curing many ailments, including dog bites, rabies and insanity, offering

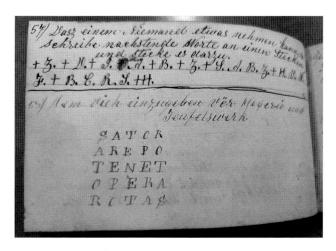

A page from Paul's book, including a Sator Square, also known as a Tenet Square. This square has often been used as a blessing or a form of prayer. One translation of the words from Latin is "the Farmer Arepo works his wheels."

A picture presumed to be of J.W.S. Paul. It is included with his spell book in the Dayton Room at the Dayton Metro Library Downtown.

medical treatments and providing relief during childbirth. Paul had his own version of a spell book along with a list of customers from Germantown he helped over the years. Paternoster, as opposed to witchcraft, is operated in tandem with Christian beliefs and uses the spells as a form of prayer. His small handwritten book, which he titled *Book of Charms for Healing*, is full of spells mostly written in German and centering on healing and positivity. There were no spells to harm or cause negativity toward anyone.

JERSEY ANGEL

In the late 1800s, a man from England came to Yellow Springs to buy some land that today is John Bryan Park. Joseph S. Saberton didn't really fit in with the other residents of Yellow Springs, partly because he was an immigrant and partly because of the different way he treated his livestock. He came from the Isle of Jersey with the first herd of Jersey cows ever in Ohio. Jersey cows are the smallest of the breed so locals ridiculed Saberton for his "pets," especially since he gave them all names. They nicknamed him the "Jersey Angel." Despite the ridicule Saberton received, his cows proved to be an excellent breed, outproducing the local shorthorn cows common to the area. When Saberton was suddenly struck with illness, he asked to be buried in the cattle field with his Jersey cows and his neighbors obliged. Since there was nobody to take over his herd, his cattle were sold off. His field stood empty for a while until his brother came to dig him up and take him out west to be buried. Not long after, a man named John Applegate and his brother Bert rented the farm. Exactly two years after the disinterment of Saberton, his ghost appeared. The Applegate brothers were standing on their porch smoking cigarettes and staring into the night. They suddenly heard a man on a horse whistling for his dog. They stood stunned as they recognized Saberton's voice and the sounds of a man on horseback riding along with his cattle. Although they didn't see anyone, the sounds were unmistakable. When folks laughed at John's telling, he walked into town to swear his story before a notary. Bert also swore to the same story. Together, the Applegate brothers believed Yellow Springs' Jersey Angel had returned to round up his cattle one last time.

TORNADO WARNING

April 3, 1974, started as a perfect spring day in Xenia as Paul helped his mother work in the yard. Paul had the day off work at the local Kroger and he was glad for it; he could enjoy the beautiful weather. Thirsty, Paul headed inside to get some water and found his mother standing in the kitchen holding a garden trowel and frowning at the barometer on the wall. When he asked her what she was thinking about, she said she didn't like the weather. Paul replied, "What do you mean? The weather is perfect!" His mom shook her head and simply stated that she was worried about his father and changed the subject.

She turned on the TV, which was unusual for her during the day and turned it to the news. Paul thought it was odd but considered it a mystery to be solved later. They ate their pancake breakfast in silence. While eating, Paul noticed a picture of his aunt Claire in the corner of the kitchen. She'd been killed in a car accident the previous year and he sorely missed her. They'd been very close and he thought about her often. Aunt Claire was clairvoyant and often predicted events about to happen. Whatever she predicted came true.

Paul returned to work in the yard with his mother, but before they went out she turned up the volume on the TV. They could listen to it while they worked, she told him. As they worked, she stopped frequently to listen to the TV. She made the comment a few more times that she was worried about Paul's dad. He was at work at the local high school and as far as Paul knew, nothing was wrong. Paul busied himself with planting and digging. Before he knew it, it was afternoon. By about 4:00 p.m., he had stopped work and felt something was off. It took only a moment before he realized he didn't hear any birds. All the normal background noises had been replaced by silence.

Paul felt a few raindrops hit his head as his mother rushed out of the house and told him she was going to get his father. She told Paul to get the cat and go inside as she rushed to her car and peeled out of the driveway. Puzzled, Paul put the tools away in the shed. He wondered what had gotten into his mother when a familiar voice behind him told him to go inside and get in the cellar. He whirled around to see Aunt Claire standing before him.

Paul stood dumbfounded at the sight of his dead Aunt Claire, unable to move or speak. Before he had time to find his voice and respond, Aunt Claire shouted, "Move!" Spurred into action, Paul ran toward the house as a powerful gust of wind shook the trees. When he got inside, he could not find the cat. As he looked around the house he couldn't help but notice a large wall of black dust in the distance.

Again, his aunt appeared at his side. This time she was shoving the cat into his arms and pushing him toward the cellar. In his haste, Paul couldn't get the cellar door open. Aunt Claire opened the door, shoved him in and shut the door behind him. Paul ran down the stairs and hid under a large, heavy table. For what seemed like hours but was probably minutes, he hunched under the table hearing the wind roaring as it rearranged the world around him. The sound was deafening. When the storm was finally over, Paul waited a bit longer before emerging from the table to see a new world in front of him.

The cellar stairs had been destroyed so Paul used debris to climb out and survey the neighborhood. It was flat and messy. The surviving neighbors were slowly gathering outside and in the chaos, Paul helped his neighbor remove a heavy beam from on top of the man's wife's leg while still holding his cat. Paul was bleeding from dozens of tiny cuts. He started walking toward the high school, in the direction his mother had driven. As he walked, he saw debris and flat land where buildings once stood. The Kroger where he worked was leveled. When he got to the high school, buses had been thrown by the wind into the building. It seemed that nobody inside could have survived. That was all he could take. Still holding his cat, Paul fell to the ground and cried.

It was then that someone lifted Paul up and put their arms around him. It was his father. He had sheltered in place with others in an inside hallway until the storm was over. Rescue workers rounded up survivors and took them to shelters where Paul and his dad reunited with Paul's mom the next day. She had been driving to get her husband when Aunt Claire appeared in the seat next to her and told her that she needed to drive out of town immediately. Claire gave her very specific turn-by-turn directions then said she had to go help Paul. It was then that Claire appeared to Paul and helped him into the cellar. Paul's mom had to beg to be allowed to come back into Xenia to find her husband and son. She had searched at three shelters before finding them. When Paul and his parents returned to the wreckage that was once their home, they found the framed picture of Aunt Claire in the rubble, untouched by the storm.

The winds of the 1974 Xenia F5 tornado reached three hundred miles an hour and damaged or destroyed more than 1,400 buildings, including 1,200 homes, dozens of businesses, 10 churches and several schools. The damage was estimated at more than $100 million. More than 1,300 people were injured and 33 killed, a number that could have been higher by 2 if not for Aunt Claire.

10

SCHOOL SPIRITS

SINCLAIR COMMUNITY COLLEGE

David Sinclair noticed a problem in the Dayton area. Although there were unemployed men and employers with job openings, they were not matching up. Sinclair took it upon himself to sit with employers and the unemployed men in the area and find out why. He determined lack of skills and knowledge to be the issue. Through Sinclair's hard work and dogged determination, mechanical drawing and bookkeeping classes were offered, helping to fill the gap. Sinclair didn't stop there, running himself ragged to expand the project and continue his mission. Although he died before seeing his project completed, Sinclair's first building was opened in 1908. Today, Sinclair Community College has locations in Englewood, Dayton, Centerville, Mason and Huber Heights. It is one of the twelve Vanguard Learning Schools, a term designated by the League for Innovation in the Community College to recognize the top twelve two-year institutions in North America focusing on student access and success.

Security Guard

As he was making his rounds one morning, the security guard couldn't believe his eyes. His supervisor stepped off the elevator and walked into

Sinclair Community College sign.

his office, an abnormal act because this supervisor's funeral had been just days before. Although the supervisor died in the Beverly Hills Supper Club fire in Southgate, Kentucky, he continued to appear for work every morning at the same time, leaving the elevator and walking to his office. Many other employees who had known him reported seeing him around the building and during his morning walk to his office. Eventually, the employees exchanged stories with one another and realized that he had been giving them all messages. He talked to one man and told him everything would be all right and that he didn't need to worry about him anymore. After relaying messages to his coworkers, the spirit stopped appearing at Sinclair.

Blair Hall

Located in Building 2 along West Fourth Street, Blair Hall is Sinclair's theater facility. Blair Hall was named for Vincent Blair, first chairman of the Board of Trustees of Sinclair Community College. Blair Hall is said to be the most haunted building on campus. People report a smothering feeling; being poked, prodded and tugged; hearing laughing and talking when nobody is around; and the sound of mysterious music playing. In addition, elevators have been known to operate on their own. The outline of a man has been seen walking on the catwalks, and laughter has been heard coming from the empty stage. Many theater participants have affectionately nicknamed the ghost "Hamlet." There's a rumor that during construction a cat was accidentally walled up and never found. A cat meowing and scratching can be heard inside the walls. In some versions of the story, feral cats were hanging around the construction site and one worker was fed up with the cats and lured them into an area with treats and poured cement over them. During one hot summer evening when the air-conditioning was broken, the staff reported feeling a cold gust of wind throughout the theater as they were closing for the night. As they were locking the revolving door, the locking bolts popped back up and the door started spinning by itself. While this was happening, the lights were turning on and off by themselves.

Cafeteria

The cafeteria of Sinclair was built directly above the location of the old hanging grounds where criminals met their deaths. One such death was John McAfee, who was convinced by lover Hetty Shoup to poison his wife. The wife took to her bed in sickness and John told her he would care for her. Instead, he gave her an elixir to make her "feel better," but it was actually poison. She lay in bed dying, but when John decided she wasn't dying fast enough he became impatient and strangled her to death. After his wife's death, John was so disgusted with himself, his lover and his actions that he ran away. He was caught at his wife's funeral and tied up with the ropes used to lower her coffin into the ground. Before he was put to death, McAfee wrote a confessional poem warning young men about the feminine wiles of a mistress and how one could lead you astray. He was hanged as his mistress watched dispassionately from the crowd. Many students have reported feeling a chill in the cafeteria and seeing the heavy fire doors open and slam shut on their own. Some say the ghosts of hanged prisoners stick around to harass students.

Mr. Joshua

Building 13 used to be the location of the United Color Press. While the press was in business, an employee's arm got caught in the press and he bled to death. A ghost later nicknamed Mr. Joshua has been seen roaming the halls and walking through walls. After locking the building, security spotted an older man with white hair looking out the window from inside. As they searched the building for the man, Dayton Police came to assist. When three officers finally cornered the man, who was dressed in blue jeans and a white shirt, he simply turned and walked through the nearest wall. Mr. Joshua's nickname derives from an incident in which a technician was printing a long document from her computer. While waiting for the document to finish printing, she busied herself with other tasks and turned her attention from the printer. When she picked up the document, the top page read "JOSHUA" in one-inch-tall capital letters across the top. She checked her computer—the word *Joshua* was nowhere to be seen on the document file.

Man and Mule

A staff member took a utility worker to service the generators and they both saw a little old man leading a mule. Before they could react, the man and his mule vanished before their eyes. Visitors have also heard the sound of a donkey braying and a man calling for her. Building 13 was formerly the location of a railroad roundhouse, a circular or semicircular building used for storing and servicing trains before it was the United Color Press. The mules were used to turn around the railroad engines. The man and his mule are believed to have died in the 1913 flood, which killed 467 people, 1,420 horses and 2,000 other animals.

STIVERS

Beware of the teacher's pet, especially if you are the teacher. At Stivers School of the Arts, Mary Tyler was the favorite faculty member of the students. She was considered to be close with many students especially one senior boy who was her senior student aide. Rumors circulated there was more than a teacher-student relationship between the two but there was no evidence of such. Despite the lack of proof, people still talked.

One day, Mary's lifeless body was discovered floating facedown in the school's Olympic-sized swimming pool. She regularly swam laps on Fridays but this time she was fully dressed. In one hand was a broken pointer; in the other was a locket containing two pictures. One picture was of her parents. The other picture was of a man and it was torn off at the head to obscure his identity. The student aide was immediately suspected of killing Mary and ripping his face from the picture but he was nowhere to be found. He never returned to school and was never heard from again, furthering suspicion of his guilt. Mary's murder was never solved.

Not long after, wood planks were laid across the sixteen-by-thirty-foot pool then covered with linoleum. A classroom was built directly over the swimming pool, leaving only a trapdoor for access. In this basement classroom, students consistently feel cold and often wear coats to class. Students and staff often hear their names being called, lights turning on and off, objects disappearing, doors opening and shutting on their own and mysterious noises when the classroom is locked for the night. Some

Stivers School for the Arts.

students have even seen the apparition of a woman. The teachers who have used the classroom have reported objects being moved around on their desks and the TV turning on and off when no one is touching it. Although most of the sightings are in the classroom above the swimming pool, the woman has been seen in other areas in the lower levels of the building. The female apparition has been described as all white with long hair, dripping wet and glowing. The sound of high heels clicking has also been heard echoing in the empty hallway. These sightings and experiences have been reported for over one hundred years. Perhaps Mary Tyler is waiting for her lover to return, penitent for his crime. Or perhaps she waits for justice.

ANTIOCH

Dodd Hall at Antioch Midwest in Yellow Springs is haunted by the ghost of a little boy who likes to jump on students in the middle of the night. The spirit is playful but has pushed students down in their beds. He has also been known to grab hands and try to hold them. In the Main Building, doors swing open and closed on their own. In the Science Building a janitor once witnessed all the doors on the third floor open and close by themselves. Misty figures have been seen floating through G Stanley Hall.

UNIVERSITY OF DAYTON

Located next to Woodland Cemetery, it is not surprising to learn that the University of Dayton has a few ghosts of its own. Some of the sightings are described in this section.

Chapel of Immaculate Conception

The apparition of a priest with several students has been seen near the building. In the 1850s, the site was St. Mary's School for Boys.

Theta Phi Alpha House

This sorority house is haunted by the ghost of a young man but his story is unknown. Several sorority sisters who lived in the house have reported seeing the apparition of this young man. Furniture and other heavy items have been moved. Residents have seen lights turning on and off, felt an ominous presence just before going to bed, and experienced extreme cold at night. Many have also reported waking up feeling drained, having less energy than they had before they went to bed the previous night. Many personal items are moved only to be returned a few days later.

Around Campus

A tall, mysterious figure in a dark cloak was spotted numerous times in the 1950s and 1960s in different parts of the campus. A student disappeared from campus around this time and the disappearance was blamed on the cloaked figure.

Liberty Hall

An old man with broken teeth and a limp walks the halls. Some who have seen this ghost believe he had a stroke that caused him to walk the way he does. Liberty Hall was once an infirmary for students and faculty so this man may have been a former patient, as many have died there. The man has also been spotted looking out the window by witnesses outside the building. A witness working in the building saw a pant leg and a dress shoe of what appeared to be a man. Liberty Hall has since been turned into offices.

St. Mary's Hall

Unnatural (or supernatural) chills and cold spots have been felt in the attic.

St. Joseph Hall

On the fourth floor of St Joseph Hall, ghostly sounds have been reported.

11

PARANORMAL PARKS

HILLS AND DALES TOWER

A building of many names, the tower on Patterson Boulevard in Kettering near Hills and Dales Park has been the source of many stories over the years. Generations of Kettering residents have explored this tower seeking out ghostly activity.

For decades, the information about this structure was not well known. Even the true name of the tower has been debated. Some of the more popular names have been:

Lookout Tower
Frankenstein's Castle/Tower
Witch's Tower
Haunted Tower/Castle
Patterson Tower
Hills and Dales Tower

The theories of its age, origin and the hauntings vary as much as its name. Teenagers in Kettering have shared many rumors about the tower and its past. One far-fetched theory was that the tower was built during the Civil War over burial grounds and the ghost was a woman who had climbed to the top and plunged to her death after learning that her husband would

Hills and Dales Tower, known by many names.

not be returning from war. She can be seen at night walking through the trees wearing a long, dark robe and looking over the edge from the top of the tower, staring into the darkness. A black mist has been reported hanging over the area surrounding the tower, its looming presence scaring away curious teenagers.

The most popular theory says that teenagers who sought shelter from an electrical storm were killed when lightning struck the tower. The outline of their bodies can be seen in the tower. On stormy nights, one can see teenagers running to the tower seeking shelter. The legends and stories of this tower persisted to the point that Kettering has shut down access to it and police patrol the area at night to deter teens from going there.

So, what is the truth? Newspaper articles verify that there was one death in the tower, that of a young lady. On May 27, 1967, Peggy Harmeson and her boyfriend, Ronnie Stevens, sought shelter from the rain. Lightning struck the tower, killing Peggy and knocking Ronnie unconscious. It was believed that in her wet clothes, Peggy had leaned against the wall, providing a route for the electricity from lightning that struck the tower through her body. Ronnie's groans attracted the attention of an assistant scoutmaster named Laurel Pearson who was walking through the area an hour later. She drove to a phone and called the police. Ronnie had been delirious when Pearson discovered him but was out of control by the time the police arrived. He had to be restrained with handcuffs in order to be loaded into the ambulance and taken to Kettering Hospital, where he was treated. Ronnie later joined the military and served in Vietnam from 1968 to 1972. He died in 1991 at age forty-one.

Peggy was buried in Calvary Cemetery after a funeral service at Immaculate Conception Church in Centerville. Peggy was very loved and one of her friends wrote a poem in her honor:

Ode to Peggy

Death. It happens every day,
But not to so many as it did this way.
In memory of a girl I knew well,
This is my story I'd like to tell.
All of this happened during a storm,
And to this couple they were not warned.
Through the sky the lightning flashed,
Then to the ground their bodies crashed.
Although we do not understand,
God has taken her from this land.
Peggy was so young and fair,
Down her back flowed long blonde hair.
Ronnie also was thoughtful and kind,
He'll never forget her in his mind.
And now the time has come for them to part,

But there'll always be a place for her in his heart.
Yes, Peggy was the unfortunate one,
Our God has taken at last a loved one,
We will not forget her always,
In our hearts or in the hallways.
To her friends and family, let them not grieve,
For one day too, they must leave.
And so, dear God, her soul do bless,
Let her lie in peace and at rest.
Till one fine day when they meet again,
They'll start a beginning and there'll be no end.
And by this death a message was sent for Peggy to come.
And now that I'm done, it may all be summed,
May we think of her as leaving this imperfect
To that all perfect and glorious home above.
Where God presides—
To the golden gates, she now arrives.

Construction on the Hills and Dales Tower was started in 1940 by the National Youth Administration. Salvaged stone of condemned buildings in the Dayton area was used as building material. The project lasted a year and resulted in a tower fifty-six feet high (with the roof) with three-foot-thick walls. The roof has since been removed, and the building is sealed shut to prevent the curious from going inside.

Maybe the true story of Hills and Dales Tower is not so scary or sensational, but that won't stop teenagers and adults alike from driving past the tower at night, hoping to see an ethereal being that fulfills the version of the ghost story they like best.

STUBBS PARK MONKEY HOUSE

Earl "Monkey" Miller opened the Monkey House to attract customers to his general store. This hexagonal building was located on the northeast corner of Whipp and Far Hills, near where Lee's Chicken is located now. Unfortunately, the first troop of monkeys did not have the best conditions and they died quickly. The next troop did better and attracted crowds. When Miller died in 1985, some of his monkeys were forgotten in the aftermath.

Again, monkeys died in the monkey house. After the house was moved to its current location in Leonard Stubbs Park, reports of activity inside the monkey house started. Hoots, squeals, and grunts sounding like monkey calls have been heard near the building and dogs walking near the building react as if they hear the sounds of monkeys inside.

JOHN BRYAN STATE PARK

The ghost of a man is said to walk the area around the west gate whistling. He wears overalls and a blue shirt and has a red handkerchief tied around his neck. The ghost is believed to be a man named Wiley the Hermit, who sold produce and soda to travelers passing through the area. He and his horse died in 1912 when they fell in the river and drowned.

GLEN HELEN, YELLOW SPRINGS

Sightings include the ghosts of several Native Americans and a young woman deemed to be Helen, whose father named the park for her after she died.

LIBRARY PARK

When Hill Grove Cemetery opened in 1863, it was decided that the interred bodies at Village Cemetery (aka Miamisburg Cemetery and later known as Library Park) would be exhumed and moved down the road to the new cemetery. This process was not a quick one, however. Families were to be responsible for moving their loved ones' remains from one cemetery to the other, but they did not hurry. In some cases, this was due to a lack of money. In others, family members were unable to be located quickly.

This lackadaisical reinterment continued until the otherworldly appearances of a young woman began. Every night at nine o'clock, she could be seen walking through the cemetery as if deep in thought. Her nightly appearances were so punctual that one could set a watch by her arrival. The number of sightings of this young lady set a record for the most

One of the picturesque attractions in Library Park.

ghostly sightings in one location in Ohio. She could be seen walking among the tombstones, unbothered by the world around her.

The sightings soon became bothersome to the residents of Miamisburg. Tourists came to town to see the nightly specter. Their presence, along with the regular appearances of the ghost, upset those living nearby. Graves were moved down the road faster, especially the graves of the Buss family. Many thought the ghost was a young Buss family member who may have been murdered. Some residents even claimed to recognize the girl.

Moving the graves did not change the nightly appearances and residents became frustrated, culminating in a town riot. Locals brought sticks, clubs, guns and stones to assault the specter but did not succeed in perturbing her.

A March 27, 1884 article* in the *Daily News* of Frederick, Maryland, gave more detail:

> *A thousand people surround the graveyard in Miamisburg, a town near Dayton, O., every night to witness the antics of what appears to be a genuine ghost. There is no doubt about the existence of the apparition, as Mayor Marshall, the revenue collector and prominent citizens testify to having seen it. Last night several hundred people, armed with clubs and guns, assaulted the specter, which appeared to be a woman in white. Clubs, bullets, and shot tore the air in which the mystic figure floated without disconcerting it in the least. The town turned out en masse today and began exhuming all the bodies in the cemetery.*
>
> *The remains of the Buss family, composed of three people, have already been exhumed. The town is visited daily by hundreds of strangers and none are disappointed, as the apparition is always on duty promptly at 9 o'clock. The strange figure was at once recognized by the inhabitants of the town as a young lady supposed to have been murdered several years ago. Her attitude while drifting among the graves is one of deep thought, with the head inclined forward and the hands clasped behind.*

The following morning, the remaining graves in the cemetery were exhumed and moved down the road to Hill Grove Cemetery.

Does Miamisburg's celebrity ghost still haunt Library Park? Sightings continued sporadically over the next one hundred years until the last confirmed sighting in the 1980s.

---

* This article appeared almost verbatim in dozens of newspapers across the United States in 1884. The one variation was the spelling of the family name, which appeared as Buss, Vuss and Nuss. The letters V, B and N are next to each other on a typical QWERTY keyboard.

CANDLEWOOD PARK (JANE NEWCOM PARK)

A boy who hanged himself in the restroom haunts the park. Three small kids were reportedly murdered in the park and their killer still haunts the area. To draw the murderer out, one must sit on the ground and draw around one's self with chalk like a body outline. Ghostly screams can be heard at night.

HELKE PARK

Located in a neighborhood in Vandalia, Helke Park boasts play structures for kids from ages two to twelve, tennis courts, softball fields, pickleball courts, volleyball courts and a new disc golf course. There are four acres of open field and a wooded area. Among the fields and greenery, the park also hosts a spirit or two. A mother visiting the park had taken pictures of her children playing. When she reviewed her pictures later, her children were surrounded by orbs. In the midst of the orbs, a ghostly child's face could be seen. A little girl has been spotted asking for help but disappears as soon as the person looks away. She has been seen by many park-goers and is commonly heard laughing. A group of a few friends took a Ouija board to the park and communicated with a spirit who identified herself as Emily. She said she died in an accident in the park in the 1930s. Another rumor has it that Emily was murdered in the 1970s.

MAGEE PARK

Real estate is all about location. Is that the case for supernatural activity as well? Magee Park in Bellbrook is the site of many supernatural events. Located smack dab in the middle of a city known as Ohio's Sleepy Hollow for the amount of ghostly activity and strange legends, Magee Park boasts more spooky stories than what can be told around a campfire in one night. Ghostly activity at this park is said to increase in June, so plan your visit for the summer.

Magee Park is home to many supernatural stories.

Woman and Her Baby

One of the first stories associated with Magee Park was that of a woman and her baby. As the legend goes, around the 1880s, a young servant girl had an affair with her master, the mayor of Bellbrook. As one can imagine, she soon found herself pregnant. When her lover discovered this, he was horrified and turned her away from his home and into the streets, hoping to hide his deed. She no longer had a job or a home; he refused to see her again. The mayor told his wife that the servant girl had gotten herself into trouble and he had kicked her out of the house. In desperation, the young woman turned to prostitution to feed herself and the baby growing inside her.

When the baby was born, the midwife said it looked just like its father. Despite what the man had done to her, the young woman wouldn't betray him and reveal his identity. She walked the streets alone at night carrying a small bundle wrapped in blankets in her arms. She wouldn't let anyone see the baby and rumors circulated that it bore such a strong resemblance to its father that one look would reveal its paternity. Instead she walked alone, ignoring the whispers as she sang a soft lullaby to her baby. Any money she was able to get she used to feed her baby. She grew thin, almost skeletal.

Finally the young mother couldn't take the whispers anymore. She went to her former lover's home to beg him for help for her and their baby. She hoped that the baby's resemblance to him would turn his heart. Unfortunately, she didn't get that chance. The servant who answered the door was ordered to slam the door in her face before she could see the father.

The rejection was devastating. The poor girl walked along the road crying and feeling more alone than ever. Her last attempt to take care of herself and her baby had failed. She walked to the bridge overlooking Little Sugar Creek (formerly Possum Creek). As she stood there heartbroken, she softly sang to her baby. She finally figured out what she was going to do. Closing her eyes, she plunged herself into the water below, her wrapped bundle held tightly in her arms.

When her body was found a few days later, the woman was still clutching a wad of blankets in her arms. But when those who found her body pulled back the cloth, they saw no baby. No baby was found anywhere near the area in the next few weeks. Was it lost in the water? Was there ever a baby at all? Nobody can say for sure, but visitors to the part of the creek where Magee Park is now located report seeing an ethereal woman walking along the bank crooning a soft lullaby to a bundle wrapped tightly in her arms.

John Buckley

In the summer of 1828, John Buckley came from London, England, and bought a small sawmill along Possum Run Creek near present-day Magee Park. He was a hard worker and ran his mill day and night. Establishing the first sawmill in the Bellbrook area made him very successful. John had money at a time when most people in the area bartered to get the things they needed. Neighbors described him as a kind and cheerful man, ready to do a kindness for anyone. Buckley was a widower living in a two-story log cabin with his three children, Mary, John and William.

According to a newspaper article published on April 24, 1901, Mr. Buckley's neighbors had a conversation with him one night after dinner as they were heading to Bellbrook. Journeying home later that evening, they discovered Buckley's body lying along the side of a log with his scalp split open. There was no way to help him as he was already dead. Not knowing what to do with his body, his neighbors carried him to his front porch and laid him down. They later buried him in the old graveyard on Possum Run Road. In an attempt to find his gold and/or silver, neighbors greedily dug up his cellar but found nothing.

Buckley's cabin stood empty for a while; nobody wanted to move into a haunted house. When it was finally rented out to a Bellbrook couple, they reported hearing noises both upstairs and in the cellar. The reports culminated with the lady of the house seeing Buckley's ghost standing in the cellar with his head cut open and bleeding. She ran from the house screaming. It did not take long for the couple to move out. As no one in the Bellbrook area would rent the house, the landlord found a tenant from Dayton. The tenant was a skeptic and went searching for answers when he heard noises. In the attic he found a large colony of rats and cleared them out. He reported hearing no more unusual sounds or noises after that. He also said he never saw a ghost. Nobody ever found John Buckley's treasure but his ghost can be seen walking the banks along the creek.

The Unnamed Miller

Not to be confused with John Buckley, another miller came to Bellbrook from Germany. This miller owned a prosperous grain and wheat mill and reportedly buried his money on his property. One night while the miller was home alone and his wife was tending to the mill, a robber broke into their home. The intruder beat the miller to death using an old log chain. For years the miller's widow hunted and dug for the money, but to no avail. It was thought to be worth $20,000. Years later, a convict in the Ohio Penitentiary confessed to the crime but said he also never found the money. This legend resulted in amateur treasure hunters visiting the scene in attempts to strike gold.

The widow eventually abandoned the home and this resulted in a revolving door of families renting the house. Ultimately, each family moved out in a hurry. Although the families changed, the stories stayed the same. Strange cries were heard from the attic as well as clanking sounds, as if a chain was being dragged across the floor. The stories were so prolific that the house eventually stood empty, unable to be rented out. It remained empty for years, visited only by thrill-seeking children and teens looking for a ghost or treasure. The house eventually collapsed and the debris was removed. The only trace of the miller and his home is his ghost, appearing just long enough to scare away anyone who dares to dig for his money.

Unicorn

Two teens hunting for squirrels noticed a strange creature drinking from the creek, and they went running home. They later described the creature as a large, pure-white beast with a horn on its head and a flowing tail. The animal was not there when they returned but it became common for locals to search for the unicorn every Sunday after church. Sightings were reported into the early 1900s.

Bigfoot

Several sightings of Bigfoot have been reported in Magee Park. In a YouTube video exploring Magee Park after dark, Project Paranormal states that Bellbrook, especially Magee Park, is in the path of the Bigfoot Migratory Route to the north. According to the Bigfoot Field Researchers Organization (BFRO), Ohio ranks fourth in the nation for what BFRO considers credible sightings or occurrences of Bigfoot, 318 as of August 27, 2022. Visitors to Magee Park have reported hearing a growling noise, known as the "Ohio Growl," among other noises in the park. Physical remnants of branches and brush associated with Bigfoot activity have also been sighted.

The Tall Man

A tall man with a skull for a face has been seen walking the creek at Magee Park. Before people see him, they get a sinking feeling in their stomach, a sense of dread.

PATTY'S HOUSE, ENGLEWOOD METROPARK

Patty Falls was named after the Patty family, who settled in the area. If you hike to the falls, you may see the remains of the house nearby. You may also see the figures of two young women hanging from the trees. According to legend, the Patty sisters were attacked and hanged in a nearby tree by an angry relative. Their screams can still be heard to this day. Park rangers have seen people walking through the woods wearing old-fashioned clothing; then they disappear. Sometimes, a noose is seen hanging from a tree and an eerie stillness pervades.

MIAMISBURG MOUND CROP CIRCLES

Miamisburg Mound is the largest conical burial mound in the eastern United States and one of the largest in the nation. It was constructed roughly two thousand years ago by the Adena people and is about seven stories high (65 feet). It is 800 feet around and contains 54,000 cubic feet of dirt. Although it has not been thoroughly excavated and examined, it is believed to be a burial mound.

When a mysterious crop-circle formation was discovered in a field near Miamisburg Mound on September 1, 2004, crop-circle investigators flocked to Miamisburg to investigate and document the results. The formation from end to end was measured at 220 feet. It was created in a field of maize (corn) 8 feet tall and all the stalks swirled clockwise. The stalks were lying down but not broken and the roots were still intact and attached. An absence of scuff marks or drag marks on the ground indicated that no machine was used to make the impressions. Based on the gravitropism of the stalks (the effect of gravity on the root growth of the stalks), the formation was at least a week old. In each of the circles, one stalk of corn was left standing in the center. The investigators determined that this was an important detail but were unsure of what it meant.

Many in the crop-circle investigation community believe there is a correlation between the Miamisburg Mound formation and one discovered a year before, in August 2003, near Serpent Mound. When the Serpent Mound and Miamisburg Mound formations are overlapped, they align to make one image. To ciriologists (crop-circle specialists), this has significance. It's also important to note that most crop circles appear near ancient or sacred burial mounds.

Just a few months prior to the Miamisburg incident, about ten miles from the site of the circles in Centerville, 911 received about ten calls from residents experiencing various electrical issues on their streets. The calls started with complaints of bright flashes of lights and strange noises. Others called in to report seeing strange objects. One caller reported seeing a UFO near power lines. Police went out to investigate but saw nothing. They decided not to investigate further, assuming the incidents were the result of a transformer issue.

Many believe crop circles are a hoax. Two gentlemen came forward in the 1980s and confessed to creating many as a prank. After that, many others shared ways they had enacted the same prank. Despite the admissions, crop circles have continued to defy explanation and evidence has not been able to establish known methods for each formation. Crop circles have been documented since the 1600s and the advancement of investigation methods and technology has far outpaced the rate of crop-circle hoax creations.

Were the 911 calls in Centerville related to the crop circles ten miles away at Miamisburg Mound? Are crop circles a real phenomenon? To nonbelievers, no explanation is possible. To believers, no explanation is necessary.

12

HAUNTED HOUSES

PATTERSON HOMESTEAD

If there is a house that can be associated with Dayton history, it's Patterson Homestead. One can't learn about the city's history without learning about the Patterson family.

Patterson Homestead was built as a three-story brick farmhouse with a sawmill and farmland in 1816 by Colonel Robert Patterson. Colonel Patterson was a Revolutionary War veteran and the founder of Lexington, Kentucky. At the time of Patterson's death in 1827, Rubicon Farm, the name of Patterson Homestead at the time, comprised 2,038 acres. Patterson must have intended to settle for life in this home, as he named it Rubicon, a reference to the expression "crossing the Rubicon," meaning passing the point of no return. The expression derives from Julius Caesar's crossing of the Rubicon River in 49 BC, beginning a civil war.

Robert's son Jefferson Patterson and his wife, Julia Johnston Patterson, inherited the house, which saw many tragedies. Their daughter Elizabeth died at age eight in 1849. Typhoid fever was the suspected cause of death. Jefferson died in 1863, and the next day his daughter Kate died at age seventeen in Cincinnati. Their double funeral was held at the house. Jefferson's son William, twenty-six, died in 1865 from Civil War–related injuries. Sixteen-year-old Stewart died in 1868. It was suspected he died of typhoid fever, as Elizabeth had. After Stewart's death, the family suspected that Elizabeth and

Patterson Homestead.

Stewart had drunk water contaminated with sewage runoff from the asylum on Wilmington Pike. They moved to a new house downtown.

Two of Jefferson and Julia's remaining sons, Frank J. and John H., founded National Cash Register (NCR). John H. married Katharine Beck and they had two children, Frederick and Dorothy. Dorothy Lane in Kettering and Moraine, where she enjoyed riding her horse, is named after her. Frank married Julia Shaw and together they had Frank S., Mary and Jefferson. Later in life, Julia Shaw Patterson Carnell would help establish the Dayton Art Institute and found the Dayton Foundation. Frank Stuart "Stu" Patterson died in a plane crash while testing military aircraft at Wright Field in 1918. Wright-Patterson Air Force Base is partially named in his honor.

It was Frank, Julia Shaw and their son Jefferson who preserved Patterson Homestead to be used as a dorm for female NCR employees and as a summer home for Julia Johnston Patterson. In 1953, Jefferson Patterson presented the home to the city. It is now managed and maintained by the Montgomery County Historical Society.

Many of the members of the Patterson family are thought to haunt Patterson Homestead, as if attending a supernatural family reunion. The staff has reported many strange occurrences while working in the house. Cold spots and items moved around are commonplace events. Rocking chairs rock on their own, and Mrs. Patterson's room is always cold. The smell of green beans, cookies and home-cooked meals emanates from a kitchen that has not been used in years. The laughter of children echoes through the house, and a ghost locked one of the volunteers in the kitchen. A psychic once visited the house and sensed a mother rocking a sick child. One of the more notable ghosts is that of a man wearing a military uniform. The sound of heavy boots walking up the stairs and the sight of a pair of legs wearing boots have been reported. During tours, an apparition of a man wearing a military-style uniform has been seen walking up the stairs to the third floor, which is off-limits to tour groups.

The people who have seen the third-floor ghost suspect him to be either Stu Patterson, who died testing military aircraft, or Robert Patterson, who fought in the Revolutionary War. Regardless, the Patterson family has chosen to gather once again at their beloved homestead.

BRADFORD HOUSE

The Robert Bradford House is a simple Federal-style two-story brick house. It was built in 1839 and Robert lived there with his wife until 1844. Residents of the house believe that Robert's wife, Elizabeth, haunts it. They attribute any unusual noises or activity to her ghost. Just after moving in, the owner was awakened to the sound of an entire china cabinet filled with dishes pushed down the stairs including the sound of dishes breaking. Tired, they decided to clean up the mess in the morning. The next morning, nothing was broken or out of place.

HAWTHORN HILL

In Oakwood, the mansion known as Hawthorn Hill sits atop a hill at 901 Harman Avenue. Originally, Orville and Wilbur Wright planned for the mansion to be shared between them, but unfortunately Wilbur died in 1912 before construction of the house was completed in 1914. Instead, their father Milton, sister Katharine and Orville moved into the house.

Wilbur and Orville hired the architectural firm Schenck and Williams to help them realize their plans for Hawthorn Hill, which was named for the hawthorn trees on the property. Orville designed some of the mechanical features of the house, such as the water storage tank and the central vacuum system. The house was the gathering place for notables of American aviation. After Orville's death, NCR owned the house until 2006, when the company donated the home to the Wright Family Foundation in honor of Orville's 135th birthday and National Aviation Day.

In the Wright family, parents Susan and Milton had their hands full with seven children; Reuchlin, Lorin, Wilbur, twins Ida and Otis (who died in infancy), Orville and the baby of the family (who shared a birthday with Orville), Katharine. When Susan Koerner Wright died of tuberculosis in 1889, Katharine took over the duties of the household as the only living female child. At fifteen, Katharine was already caring for her father and four older brothers. She was especially close to Wilbur and Orville, working closely with them and even accompanying them on many of their trips. After Milton's death, Katharine and Orville grew closer and Orville couldn't imagine his life without his sister. When she got married to college friend Henry Haskell, Orville refused to speak to her. Katharine was devastated at the deterioration of her relationship with her brother. Two years later, she contracted pneumonia. Lorin was finally able to convince Orville to reconnect with Katharine. Orville was by her side when she died at age fifty-four.

Perhaps all her time in the house and her relationship with Orville has kept Katharine's spirit in Dayton. When her bedroom set from Hawthorn Hill was on display in the Old Courthouse, an apparition resembling Katharine was spotted peering out the window of the building. Although they would make her bed and pull the top sheet flat, caretakers would come back to find the bed looking as if someone had slept in it. The bedroom set has since been moved back to Hawthorn Hill and the activity has resumed there. The bedspread continues to look as if someone had just been in it despite it being smoothed many times. Heavy doors open and close by themselves and a ghostly woman is seen peering out of the mansion's windows. A large ghostly dog has been seen roaming the grounds as well, likely Scipio, Orville's treasured St. Bernard. Orville loved Scipio so much that he carried a picture of the dog in his wallet until his death in 1948, twenty-four years after the death of Scipio.

Orville had a touch of psychic ability and sometimes had premonitions. One such premonition took place while Orville and Wilbur were living on

North Summit Street, a house lit by gas. Orville was home in bed but not sleeping yet and he had a premonition that when Wilbur got home he would turn off the light but not the gas and they would suffocate in their sleep. When Wilbur got home, turned off the lights and went to bed, Orville snuck out of bed and checked. Sure enough, Wilbur had just turned off the light, and the house was already filling with gas.

Orville also liked to joke about his gift. During a visit, Griffith Brewer, president of the Aeronautical Society of Great Britain, quoted a line of poetry that Orville really liked. Orville asked who wrote it but Brewer could not remember the name. Together they looked through all of Orville's books of quotations but couldn't find the source. By coincidence the next day, Orville received a letter from a man who quoted that exact line and gave the source, Book VI of Milton's *Paradise Lost*. Orville located the lines in his copy of that book and replaced it on his shelf. It stuck out just a bit beyond the books next to it. He then called Brewer to come back to the house, telling him he would use his psychic gift to identify the author and quote. Brewer blindfolded Orville and led him to the library. Orville felt his way through to the book sticking out ever so slightly. He told Brewer he had a feeling this was the right book and Brewer removed his blindfold. Orville then opened the book to the exact page and located the quote. Brewer went to his grave believing Orville was psychic.

BERRYHILL-MORRIS HOUSE

This historic Bellbrook farmhouse was built in the 1830s for a Revolutionary War veteran, Alexander Berryhill. When he and his wife Rachel moved to Ohio they became one of the pioneer families in Bellbrook. Their son Samuel took over the farm then later the Morris family bought the property and gave it the other half of its name. While the Berryhills lived in the house, two young boys died there from cholera. Since that time, despite being occupied, no children have been born to residents of the home while they live there. The sounds of children laughing and running have been reported and visitors feel an eerie sensation as if someone is in the room with them.

ANGRY GHOSTS

On a calm winter night in 1892, Edward Wallace was sitting with his wife and their five children in a room in their small log house near the railroad tracks in Waynesville. The night was peaceful and relaxing as they busied themselves with their own tasks. The quiet was interrupted when a ghost suddenly appeared before them. At once, the spirit blew out their lights and demanded they leave the house and never return. Confused, the family members protested this idea. When they did, the ghost grabbed the nearest child, the oldest, Cora. He quickly shoved her facedown onto the nearby table and started beating her. In shock, the family members could only watch in horror, glued to their seats. They recognized the ghost as that of Joe Lynch, who was murdered in 1878 in Waynesville by James Buckner. Before they had time to wonder why he showed up or react to his actions, another ghost appeared and rescued Cora. As the second ghost started fighting the first ghost, they recognized the second spirit as the ghost of their relative Warren Cotton. Warren had died only a few years after Joe Lynch, but as far as the family knew, Lynch and Cotton had never met. The Wallace family had also never met Joe Lynch.

The appearance of Warren Cotton's ghost started an epic supernatural battle. The ghosts screamed like banshees, their eyes gleaming in the darkness and the atmosphere was charged with electricity. Furniture tumbled to the floor, chairs were broken and objects flew about the room as the spirits fought. As the glass from shattered windows scattered about the room, the action became too much to bear. The Wallace family fled in terror leaving all their possessions behind in the ghostly battleground that was their house. As they fled, they told a neighbor they had been run from their house by the ghost of a murdered man.

When they arrived in Xenia at the home of their friend Archie Valentine, they were almost incoherent with terror. It was late at night as they related the story to him, breathless. Valentine, living in an area known as Barr's Bottom, already had a large family in his small house but he did his best to accommodate his friend Edward Wallace and his family. He certainly wasn't going to turn them away in their time of need. Valentine didn't have to accommodate them for long though. That night as the Wallace family settled in, another spirit appeared before them telling them to move on from the house. Already on edge and hoping to avoid another ghostly battle, they did not hesitate to listen to what this spirit told them. Without giving any more information on their way out, the Wallace family quickly slipped into the darkness of the night and were never heard from again.

CHARLIE BATDORF'S HOUSE

Before Fairborn became a city, there were the cities of Fairfield and Osborn. A young man named Charlie Batdorf lived in the Fairfield area with his doting parents. Although they were sad to see him leave, they were so proud of him when he left to fight for the Union in the Civil War. Unfortunately, Charlie did not come back. In May 1864, he fought in the infamous Battle of the Wilderness, a bloody conflict in which neither the Union nor the Confederacy could claim victory. Estimated casualties for this battle were nearly thirty thousand, split almost evenly but with more on the Union side. It was during this battle that Charlie lost his life. When he did not return from war, his devastated family packed up and moved to another city.

Another family moved in, but almost immediately they started spending most of their time away visiting friends and relatives so they were often not at home. It seemed the Cox family never wanted to be at the house. When they were, they were eager to leave again. They asked their neighbors, a mother and daughter, to look after their home while they were away. Soon after the neighbors agreed to help, they regretted it. As the ladies were leaving the house after checking on things, they heard the sound of footsteps crunching on the gravel outside. When they went to see who was there they saw the boots of a soldier walking along the path to the house. Looking up from the boots, they noticed his military uniform. Their gaze continued up to see a stump where a head should be. Although the head was missing they could see the stump moving as if looking from side to side. They got the distinct impression the soldier was looking around as if to find the house. Frightened, a scream escaped from the daughter's lips. In response, the headless soldier frantically reached its arms out, trying to grab at the sound. The women ran as fast as they could and didn't stop until they reached their own home. When they were inside and the door was locked, the mother looked at her daughter and said, "That's Charlie Batdorf!" At once, they realized why their neighbors never wanted to be at home. They had seen the headless ghost of Charlie Batdorf trying to find his way home.

DEATH WON'T DO US PART

Successful banker Albert White had a large stone house built for his wife, Jane. Jane and Albert had a good marriage but she was unable to have a child.

With every year that passed that she couldn't have a child, Jane became more depressed. For treatment she was given the shock therapy, common at the time. The treatment made her worse. In time, Jane sank further into her illness. To compensate for the stress of his wife's illness, Albert drank heavily. When he died of alcoholism, it took days for neighbors to understand that Jane was asking for help. As Albert lay dead in their home, neighbors assumed Jane's ramblings were nonsense and ignored her requests for help. When they finally understood, Jane was taken away and committed.

Jane and Albert's home was sold to a Mrs. Turner. Almost immediately she heard noises in her new home, the sound of a person walking up the stairs and walking in the room above her. Turner began to study the ghost and determined that it was a male ghost, heavy, not mean. He seemed to be meandering through the house as if looking for something or waiting. He did not harm her, but she always felt as though he didn't like her being in his room. Eventually, she came to the conclusion that this was the ghost of the late Albert White. She often smelled cigar smoke and found burns on the carpet from ashes.

Mrs. Turner's daughter lived next door and often checked on her mother by popping in and by checking with her through their intercom system, set up to reassure Mrs. Turner after she began experiencing the haunting. One day while at her mother's house, Turner's daughter was finally fed up with the ghostly activity and yelled at the spirit telling him that it is no longer his house, that his wife doesn't live there anymore, and that he needs to leave. Unfortunately, this did nothing to curb the activity and it continued for five more years. One day while visiting, she made the comment to her mother that she hadn't heard of her mother experiencing anything in weeks. When the ladies realized this was true, they mentioned it to another neighbor who told them that Jane White had died a month before. Mrs. Turner never experienced any ghostly disturbances again.

The primary source for this story changed the names of everyone involved.

POUNDING PETE

A ghost nicknamed Pounding Pete knocked only for certain visitors at the J.F. Hoover household on Bower Avenue in Riverside. *Dayton Journal* reporter Chesta Fulmer took it personally when Pete wouldn't knock for her. In her article, she described visiting the house and waiting to hear the knocking only for the ghost to remain stubbornly silent. "Three different times my mother's favorite only child has parked her feet under the Hoovers' table and waited for just one little tap. It doesn't come. For all I know, this closet-clinking shade may be sitting around some ghostly table telling his proud transparent children 'Let 'er wait. She's the gal who doesn't believe in ghosts'."

When the ghost wasn't being silent, a tapping sound could be heard sporadically. At times, the tapping was loud enough to bother the neighbors, who crowded into the dining room for hours to listen for the sound. Some groups left disappointed; others were satisfied. The crowds became so much that the Hoovers roped off their yard. Mr. Hoover had taken to boring holes in the closet ceilings to find the source of the tapping but after shining a light in the holes he found no explanation. The Hoovers' toddler had no trouble getting Pounding Pete to respond and he often heard rapping responses to his delighted stomps.

13

WEIRD WRIGHT—PATTERSON

Wright-Patterson Air Force Base (WPAFB) is east of Dayton and located in both Greene and Montgomery Counties. Wright Field and Patterson Field are both located within the base. The National Museum of the United States Air Force is located at the base and is the oldest and largest military aviation museum in the world.

GHOSTS AT THE AIR FORCE MUSEUM

Black Mariah

The Sikorsky CH-3E (Cargo Helicopter) (#63-09676), known as *Black Mariah*, was used for classified missions in Vietnam. Before it was painted, it was part of a pair of helicopters sent to Nakhon Phanom Royal Thai Air Force Base, Thailand, from the Tactical Air Warfare Center at Eglin Air Force Base in Florida. The helicopters were determined to be more adequate search-and-rescue aircrafts than what was at hand and due to their green color, were nicknamed "Jolly Green Giants" by their pilots. *Black Mariah* answered under the call name "Jolly Green 2." The two Jolly Greens were returned to Tactical Air Command and joined the "Pony Express." It was there that Jolly Green 2 was painted flat black to hide the insignia on the plane and this lent it a new name, *Black Mariah*. The lights were also disconnected to

Formerly a deep green color, *Black Mariah* was painted flat black for classified missions.

prevent accidental lighting during night missions. During its time on the Pony Express, *Black Mariah* flew many support and counterinsurgency missions. Rumors circulated that the Viet Cong had a $50,000 bounty out for *Black Mariah*. The craft was riddled with bullet holes and it is not known how many soldiers died inside. If you look closely, you may see the small patches riveted to the aircraft. Visitors to this exhibit report feeling a deep sense of sadness, helplessness and fear. Many believe they are experiencing the last feelings of the soldiers who died inside *Black Mariah*. Moans and voices have also been heard coming from inside.

Strawberry Bitch

Strawberry Bitch is said to be the most haunted plane in the museum. It was painted desert pink for camouflage purposes for World War II campaigns in North Africa and flew over fifty combat missions in nine months with the 512th Bomb Squadron of the 376th BG. *Strawberry Bitch* took part in and survived the Ploesti Oil Refinery raid of August 1943. The ball turret

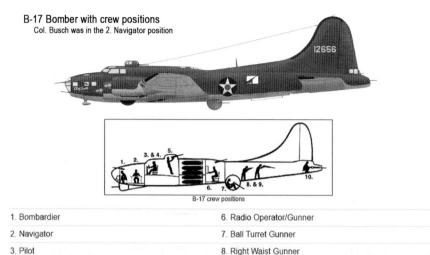

1. Bombardier	6. Radio Operator/Gunner
2. Navigator	7. Ball Turret Gunner
3. Pilot	8. Right Waist Gunner
4. Co-Pilot	9. Left Waist Gunner
5. Top Turret Gunner/Engineer	10. Tail Gunner

A diagram showing gunner locations in a military aircraft. *Public domain*.

Strawberry Bitch, believed to be the most haunted airplane at Wright Patterson Air Force Museum.

gunner position on this plane was incredibly dangerous. These gunners had to squeeze into the ball in the fetal position and use hand controls to fire the guns. The gunner would look through a small circular window between his feet. This position typically went to the smallest man on the crew, as space was limited. The ball turret was made as small as possible to reduce drag during flight and it was a very precarious position to take. It was an easy target for enemies, and if anything went wrong with the landing gear, the ball turret would take the first impact of a rough landing. The ghost of *Strawberry Bitch* may be that of a ball turret gunner who died on a mission. In this B-24, the ball turret has been removed and a ball turret sits nearby on display.

Witnesses have reported seeing guns on the plane move as if they are shooting. A janitor has also reported being slapped while near the plane and lights are spotted inside, despite no electricity being connected. Noises and clicks are heard when it's quiet.

The experience of the ball turret gunner has been summarized in the poem "The Death of the Ball Turret Gunner" by Randall Jarrell, displayed near the exhibit.

> *From my mother's sleep I fell into the State*
> *And I hunched in its belly till my wet fur froze.*
> *Six miles from earth, loosed from its dream of life,*
> *I woke to black flak and the nightmare fighters.*
> *When I died they washed me out of the turret with a hose*

Bockscar

This B-29's name, *Bockscar*, derives its spelling (not "boxcar") because it was named after its pilot, Captain Frederick Bock. When delivered to the U.S. Air Force in March 1945, the B-29 was immediately assigned to Bock. Although it was considered to be Bock's plane, a different pilot, Major Charles Sweeney, flew it when it dropped the "Fat Man" bomb on Nagasaki on August 9, 1945. Sweeney normally flew *The Great Artiste* and piloted the craft as an observation plane for the *Enola Gay* when it dropped the bomb on Hiroshima. To eliminate the need to remove and reinstall complex scientific equipment between *The Great Artiste* and *Bockscar*, Sweeney and Bock simply switched planes with *The Great Artiste*, picking up the role of observation plane once again. The target for this drop was actually the city Kokura, but

Bockscar, named for its pilot, Frederick Bock.

clouds obscured the view that day so Sweeney proceeded to the secondary target, Nagasaki.

"Fat Man" had a blast yield equal to 21 kilotons of TNT. Almost half of Nagasaki was destroyed and 35,000 people were killed and 60,000 more were injured. A crew member on *Bockscar* described the blast as feeling like the plane was being beaten by a telephone pole.

A young Japanese boy has been spotted running near the plane in the museum when there aren't a lot of people around. This boy has been seen by many staff and guests, even in the middle of the day.

Lady Be Good

In 1943, twenty-five B-24s of the 37th Bomb Group took off from their base in Libya for an attack against facilities in Naples. All but one returned that night. The one missing was *Lady Be Good*. It took nearly sixteen years for the plane to be discovered in the Libyan desert. When a ground party reached the plane in March 1959, evidence showed that the crew had gotten lost in the dark and flew over the base south into the desert. When the fuel ran out, the men attempted to walk to base from where the plane landed.

A propeller from the *Lady Be Good* plane.

A long search for the remains returned eight of the nine crew members. One was located near the plane and seven far north of the plane. Five of the crew had walked 78 miles before succumbing to the desert; one man had even gone 109 miles. Additionally, the men had lived for eight days, which was miraculously longer than the two-day survival expectation of men in those conditions. No trace of the ninth man was ever found.

The plane was disassembled and various parts were returned to the United States for study. Other parts were installed in other aircrafts. All the aircrafts with *Lady Be Good* parts have experienced significant technical difficulties resulting in crashes or emergency landings. An army "Otter" airplane with an armrest from the *Lady Be Good* crashed in the Gulf of Sidra with ten men aboard. No traces of the men were ever found. One of the very few surviving pieces of debris to wash ashore was the armrest of *Lady Be Good*.

A propeller from *Lady Be Good* is on display near *Strawberry Bitch*. The nine crew members still report for duty and are seen walking through the halls of the museum as if recreating their last journey away from the plane. Pieces of *Lady Be Good*'s wreckage displayed in the museum are known to rearrange themselves.

Hopalong

This Sikorsky UH-19B (Utility Helicopter) Chickasaw was used by medevac troops in Korea and early on in Vietnam. The craft was designed to maximize cabin space and the engine was mounted in the nose of the plane. This allowed for more room for personnel and cargo. The design also minimized the impact of different weights of cargo inside the cabin. The clamshell-style doors over the engine allowed for easier access for maintenance. This was the first of the Sikorsky helicopters with enough cabin space and lifting ability to allow satisfactory operations in troop transport and rescue roles. A hoist was installed over the cabin door with a capacity of four hundred pounds for rescue operations. *Hopalong* was one of the two H-19s to make the first transatlantic flight. The two helicopters traveled from Westover Air Force Base in Massachusetts to Scotland.

The pilot operating this aircraft on one of its last missions is said to be haunting it. A bloodstain can still be seen on the seat where he died. At night, the maintenance staff has seen him sitting in his bloodstained seat flipping switches and operating controls as if trying to get home safely.

SAM (Special Air Mission) 26000 Air Force One

During its thirty-six years of service, Boeing 7079 SAM 26000 carried eight U.S. presidents: Kennedy, Johnson, Nixon, Ford, Carter, Reagan, George H.W. Bush and George W. Bush. It also carried important political figures such as Queen Elizabeth, Secretary of State James Baker and Henry Kissinger. The plane also made many important trips, including the trip back to Washington, D.C., after Lyndon B Johnson was sworn in as president after John F. Kennedy was assassinated. The plane carried the new president and the body of the late president. The former First Lady Jacqueline Kennedy, accompanied her husband's body in transit. When it was suggested to put the late president's body below in storage for the ride, she would not hear of it. President Kennedy would not be treated as cargo. Instead, she had seats in the cabin removed so his coffin could be set out in the passenger section for the flight. JFK's apparition has been seen walking up and down the aisle in the cabin, often looking out the windows of the plane. Another ghost has been sighted, described as a classy-looking woman, poised and dignified. She is barely visible, a faint and shimmery mist. Those who have seen her describe an aura of immense grief radiating

Air Force One, which carried many famous people, living and dead.

from her. She sits looking dejected, head bowed and eyes down. Her face holds the expression of composure and intense sadness. When they see her, many look away in sympathy. Many haven't reported seeing the ghost, out of a sense of protection for her. Perhaps the ghost of Jackie O. is joining her lost husband?

POW Exhibit

As you enter the exhibit through a doorway to Hoa Lo Prison, nicknamed the Hanoi Hilton by American prisoners, you will learn about life as a prisoner of war. The term *Hoa Lo* refers to a potter's kiln but translates to "hell's hole." With walls topped with barbed wire and broken glass, escape was nearly impossible. Through videos, dioramas and photos, one can see the living conditions the POWs had to endure. One of every three American prisoners died from disease, injury or execution. As they walk through, the more sensitive visitors have reported a feeling of dread, hopelessness and utter sadness.

POW exhibit depicting the cells and living conditions at the "Hotel Hanoi."

The Boxcar

Not to be confused with the airplane called *Bockscar*, this is an actual boxcar used by the Germans to transport POWs from France to concentration camps in Germany. There was much suffering and many deaths inside the boxcar. Many who take pictures of this display have noticed orbs in the background after reviewing their photos.

Other Hauntings

Other hauntings at the Wright-Patterson museum include the ghost of a man in "pinks," or a dress uniform worn by junior- and senior-grade pilots in World War II. A ghost wearing pinks set off an alarm and when police responded, he simply waved and disappeared. Another ghost, a man in coveralls working on a C-47, once spoke to a staff member then vanished. The C-47 he was working on was gone by the next day. Visitors to the museum after hours have reported hearing hushed whispering, talking and the sounds of machine guns firing. Cold spots and lurking shadows have also been reported.

AIR FORCE BASE GHOSTS

Building 219

Building 219 in Area C is an office converted from an old hospital. In a terrifying incident, all the doors on the third floor slammed at the exact same time. In the basement, a judge advocate general's meeting was interrupted by the sound of children laughing and playing and a little boy is often seen. Many believe he was once a patient in the hospital and died there. The basement was once the location of the morgue.

Building 70

Area A's Building 70 plays host to a waxy-looking figure wearing a blue dress and a white shirt with ruffles. Electronics turning on by themselves, disembodied voices and footsteps have all been reported. Another story has an elderly woman roaming the building, calling out to people as they pass through. When the building is empty, people nearby often hear crashing sounds coming from inside.

Arnold House

The Arnold House is located near Huffman Prairie, where the Wright brothers used to work on their planes. It is now a part of Wright-Patterson Air Force Base. Although many commanders have lived in this house, it was named for its most famous resident, Henry H. Arnold. He was known as "Hap," a nickname given to him during his time at West Point Academy. Hap learned to fly directly from the Wright brothers, was commander of Army Air Forces in World War II, and contributed to most major developmental milestones of aviation. His career earned him a permanent five-star rank as general of the air force, a commission never granted before.

Visitors to the Arnold House report strange noises, unusual shadows, objects moving on their own and other disturbances. The TV show *Ghost Hunters* visited the house and determined there were at least five entities present, one of which is Hap himself. While investigating, the ghost hunters heard girls laughing in the dining room and sounds coming from the bathroom. They requested that the ghosts turn on some lights, which they did. One of the hosts was able to interact with a ghost through a series of taps responding to questions.

ALIENS AND HANGAR 18

Dayton is considered a hot spot for UFO sightings and activity. According to UFOlogists, one possibility is that the government is experimenting with supersecret experimental aircraft at Wright-Patterson Air Force Base and the aircrafts created are the sightings. Another theory is that since Dayton is the hub of aviation and aeronautics, aliens frequent the area, curious to see our progress in the field.

Roswell, New Mexico

Hangar 18 supposedly houses the bodies of aliens and debris from the Roswell wreckage from June 1947 on the air force base. As the story goes, the government brought the wreckage from Roswell to the base via a B-29. It's believed that extraterrestrial bodies and wreckage from a flying saucer were included in this transport.

A World War II veteran named Marion "Black Mac" Macgruder, a former fighter pilot, claimed to have seen an alien at WPAFB. In an interview with *UFO Magazine*, he said he was called to come to WPAFB a few weeks after the Roswell crash to give feedback on a decision that had to be made. The decision, according to Mac, was whether or not to disclose to the general public that the government had brought back not only a UFO but also a living extraterrestrial. Mac described the creature as under five feet with long arms, a large head and eyes, a small slit for a mouth and hardly any nose. It was wearing an outfit resembling a flight jumpsuit. The other items Mac saw that evening coincided with eyewitness reports from Roswell, such as I-beam structures with indecipherable writing. The creature did not live long. Mac suspected the death was a result of the testing doctors performed on it.

UFO enthusiasts believe the government hid evidence of extraterrestrial life, such as flying saucer debris, alien remains and even living aliens in a specific, highly guarded, secret location called the "Blue Room."

In the 1960s, Senator Barry Goldwater claimed he asked General Curtis LeMay if he could see the Blue Room. General LeMay not only said no, but he also told Goldwater that he should never ask again.

Aztec, New Mexico

Another crash rumored to have happened a year after the Roswell incident was in Aztec, New Mexico, on March 25, 1948. The wreckage from that crash was also rumored to have been taken to Hangar 18 at WPAFB. This crash was considered to be more secretive than the Roswell event and since all sixteen occupants of this craft were killed in the crash, the purpose of the trip and origin of the aircraft's inhabitants are unknown. The craft was roughly one hundred feet in diameter and eighteen feet tall. The contents from the crash that were supposedly sent to Hangar 18 are also unknown.

Some detractors have dismissed this incident as a hoax, a product of two con men who attempted to sell devices they called doodlebugs. They claimed the devices could help customers find gold, oil or gas. They also claimed to have recovered "alien technology" from the Aztec crash. The devices were later exposed as phony and the men were eventually convicted of fraud.

Devout UFOlogists still believe this crash happened and that because of the public's reaction to Roswell, the remnants were sent to WPAFB and the incident covered up to prevent panic. It is common belief that WPAFB receives wreckage from all UFO crashes to reverse-engineer the technology. Innovations such as fiber optics, particle beams, the integrated circuit, lasers and night vision have been attributed to the practice of reverse engineering alien technology.

In 1974, a UFOlogist from Florida named Robert Spencer Carr claimed to have had a conversation with a high-ranking military source who personally saw twelve alien bodies studied by necropsy (an autopsy performed on a nonhuman creature). The source also said the U.S. Air Force was hiding two flying saucers at Hangar 18.

Does Hangar 18 Exist?

Hangar 18 is often depicted as a huge structure with no windows storing remnants of Roswell, Aztec and subsequent extraterrestrial wreckage. The book *The Black World of UFOs: Exempt from Disclosure* theorizes that Hangar 18 is actually Hangar 23, which sits between buildings 18A and 18F. In Hangar 23, the floor was removed and the wreckage was stored in the newly dug out basement, which was connected to a series of underground tunnels.

UFO Sightings

In the past fifteen years, Ohioans have reported nearly three thousand UFO sightings, making the state eighth in the nation for UFO sightings. Here are some:

December 12, 2012, Beavercreek: Red light objects floating over Dayton
February 20, 2013, Huber Heights: Object hovering in the sky
April 8, 2014, Dayton: Star-shaped aircraft descending across I-35 then vanishing

August 4, 2016, Fairborn: Metallic pill-shaped UFO flying overhead at a
  park near WPAFB
October 16, 2017, Bellbrook: Orange lights
December 25, 2018, Miamisburg: Strange fireball light that didn't burn out
April 3, 2019, Englewood: Green ball of light in night sky
February 4, 2021, Germantown: Strange-moving, color-changing sphere
March 17, 2022, Kettering: Hovering craft coming out of nowhere then
  flying over

Project Blue Book

WPAFB led the research for Project Blue Book, a study of 12,618
UFO sightings between 1952 and 1969. Project Blue Book had two
goals: to determine if UFOs were a threat to national security and to
scientifically analyze UFO-related data. After seventeen years, the U.S.
Air Force determined:

1. None of the UFOs reported and investigated was a threat to national
   security.
2. Nothing left unidentified after investigation was determined to be of
   superior technology or beyond the range of current scientific knowledge.
3. No evidence indicated that sightings categorized as unidentified were
   extraterrestrial vehicles.

The air force concluded that most of the sightings were identified as
UFOs when they were actually just natural phenomena like clouds and
stars or conventional aircraft. Many of the other unidentified crafts could
be explained as reconnaissance planes on secret missions. The UFO reports
are available via the Freedom of Information Act. Names and personal
information of witnesses have been redacted.

14

TERRIFYING TIDBITS

S ometimes, there just isn't enough information for a story, but the idea of a ghostly presence still generates interest. What follows are stories in which not much more is known than just a few facts.

BOONSHOFT MUSEUM, DAYTON

A young woman working at Boonshoft had an admirer in the form of a male coworker. She was not interested in him and he could not handle the rejection. He followed her to work as she walked through the woods surrounding Boonshoft one morning. When he caught up to her, he sexually assaulted her, strangled her to death, then left her body on the ground. Someone reported hearing screams coming from the woods and when her coworkers realized that she didn't show up for work, they searched for her and found her body. Her ghost has been seen wandering Boonshoft at night and crying while she walks through the woods where she died.

"NEVERMORE"

A cheeky ghost speaking only one word made itself known to many members of the Xenia community in 1881. One particular group was leaving church when the ghost appeared before them, arms outstretched and stopping the group in its tracks. For a moment, the ghost and the group stood in silence, exchanging only stares. Finally, the ghost spoke and in a cryptic tone said one word, "Nevermore," then disappeared.

Another incident occurred when a blacksmith was walking home one night and encountered the same ghost on a secluded part of the path. He commanded the ghost to step out of his way but it did not listen. The blacksmith attempted to walk around it, but the ghost kept shifting into his path. Angry, the blacksmith made threats to the ghost, telling him he would shoot. When the ghost did not move, the blacksmith fired three shots. Although the gun was almost directly against the ghost's body and was aimed perfectly, the shots did not have an effect. The ghost did not flinch and as the smoke cleared and the silence returned, the ghost vanished after uttering just one word. Quoth the spirit, "Nevermore."

OREGON DISTRICT

This popular section of Fifth Street hosts many lively events and venues. It hosts many ghosts as well. Businesses in the Oregon District reported to be haunted are Blind Bob's, Tumbleweed Connection (now NextDoor), Trolley Stop, Ned Peppers and the former location of Sloopy's, along with the apartment above it. Glen Scott of Glen Scott Tattoo has also reported activity in his former shop in the Oregon. Three different ghost-hunting teams visited the shop and determined there were three ghosts: a man, a woman and a child. One of the teams brought back an associate who determined that seven ghosts were present in the shop. Employees have reported seeing something out of the corner of their eye, strange noises and a corner of a room that is always cold.

POLEN FARM, KETTERING

Mr. Polen, the namesake, was said to have committed suicide on the land and he still haunts the house and barn. Staff has reported hearing noises late at night, and guests to Polen Farm have felt cold spots.

SPITFIRE BAR, VANDALIA

The man who is reportedly haunting the bar is buried in the cemetery next door. A paranormal investigator looking into the place reported sounds and movements and gathered a lot of useful footage.

OLD VETERANS CHILDREN'S HOME, XENIA

The Old Veterans Children's Home opened in 1869 by the Grand Army of the Republic to provide a safe home for children of men who died in the Civil War. The orphanage operated from 1870 to 1997. It is now closed, but sounds of children laughing and playing are commonly reported to this day.

ENGLEWOOD LAKE

In winter, when the lake is frozen over and there is fresh snow, small boot prints appear on the ice of this lake. The size of the prints indicates that they belong to a woman and they lead to the middle of the lake, then stop. This is where the woman, when she was alive, fell through the ice and froze to death. She repeats her last steps year-round, but you can only see them when it snows.

COX ARBORETUM

While hiking on the Blue Trail, Lily* and her husband stopped to admire a tufted titmouse when they noticed someone else admiring the bird. Off in the woods they could see a monk, his hair styled in a historic tonsure (bald patch shaved into the hair, often in the middle of the scalp to create a ring of hair around it). He was wearing a robe made of a rough brown material with a cord tied around the middle. They looked at each other and the monk vanished before their eyes.

* Name changed at request of the source.

KEIFER STREET

A red-headed apparition of a woman wearing a construction hat has been spotted walking near the railroad tracks.

OLD ST. ELIZABETH HOSPITAL

The Medical Center at Elizabeth Place has been known by many names: Franciscan Medical Center, St. E's and St. Elizabeth, among others. Regardless of the name, the one thing that's constant are the ghostly guests who make this location their home. Mysterious moving shadows, cold spots, doors slamming and elevators moving up and down are par for the course. Lights turn on and off in a room where nuns used to sleep and perfume can be smelled inside. Elevators go up and down on their own, opening on floors where nobody called them. A security guard went to investigate some noises. He found nothing, then left the area. Just after he left, security cameras picked up footage of a wheelchair moving on its own from the edge of a room to the center. Once in the center, it slowly spun in a circle.

HOSPICE OF DAYTON

The inpatient unit at Hospice of Dayton reports sightings of children walking by or playing. These sightings are normally made by patients. The staff refers to the spirits as "the kids."

CLAYTON FIRE STATION 84

A ghostly little boy has been spotted running in the main hall of the station. Mysterious noises are heard at night when only one person is on duty. Doors open and close by themselves. When the noises are investigated, tools are found scattered about the floor. Objects will go missing and reappear in strange places and firefighters have seen the apparition of a little boy.

THE HEADLESS FIRESTARTER, XENIA

Seen at night starting fires on the road, this headless apparition, along with any damage from the fire, disappears with the morning light.

OHIO SALLY

Captain Tasker Brim was a quiet man who kept mostly to himself and spoke only when necessary. All that his neighbors knew about him was that he came to Yellow Springs from Cincinnati. He was a river man, they said. Although they thought it odd that a man in his forties would leave his boat and come to a city without a river, they didn't question him.

One day, he came into the saloon all smiles and called everyone to the bar to make an announcement. "I made my last payment," he said. "She's all mine now." *Ohio Sally*, as he called it, was his steamboat. As the patrons of the bar lifted their glasses to say goodbye to him, Captain Brim surprised them all by declaring that he wasn't leaving to resume his job as a steamboat captain. Instead, he was bringing his boat up to Yellow Springs.

Captain Brim had the boat disassembled and shipped to Yellow Springs, where, with the help of local carpenters, he used the lumber from the boat to build a house. He added a cupola (a tower-like structure on a roof) and painted the words *Ohio Sally* on the top. He then put the bell from the steamboat inside. Whenever there was a fog, Captain Brim rang the bell.

It wasn't until Captain Brim's death that the mystery of the steamboat came to light. Looking through his papers, his neighbors discovered that he had been engaged to a Kentucky girl named Sally. He had taken her for a ride on his boat, but an accident occurred and she drowned. This was the reason Brim retired as a captain and lived a solitary life in Yellow Springs. He built his house from the boat they were in when she drowned.

On foggy nights in Yellow Springs, one can hear the sound of the ship's bell ringing in the mist.

KNIGHTS INN, VANDALIA

Guests at the Knights Inn on Poe Avenue have heard tapping on their windows and seen the door handles shake, as if someone is trying to get in.

The sound of people running up and down the hallways is reported when nobody is seen. Doors have opened and shut on their own. Most of this activity has been reported in the rooms numbered in the 140s.

ENGINEER'S CLUB, DOWNTOWN DAYTON

Many of the rooms in the Engineer's Club have been the sites of reported activity. Maintenance workers have things thrown at them and lots of noise comes from the auditorium when it's empty. Guests in the dining room, which is considered to be the most haunted room, have felt pushed and pulled.

ZECK ROAD, MIAMISBURG

Two kids are said to have died in a barn fire and they stay around, haunting the barn. Sounds of children playing have been heard and the apparition of a man with a beard has been seen walking along Zeck Road (also spelled Zech Road).

GRANDMA'S FURNITURE, CLAYTON

After her grandmother died, Lucy* and her sister moved their grandma's bedroom set into Lucy's bedroom in their new apartment. It did not take long for spooky events to follow. Doors and cabinets opened and closed on their own and the thermostat adjusted by itself. The sisters also heard unexplained noises. One night while having company over, the sisters heard noises coming from the bedroom. A large cabinet that had been closed was found open with its contents spilled onto the floor. Their brother ran into the room with a makeshift weapon but quickly ran out when he realized there was no intruder. The sisters had a friend with some psychic ability come to the house to help. The friend told them that their grandma was behind the disturbances. Her furniture, which she owned her whole life, had never

---

* Name changed by source.

been moved from her house until the sisters moved the pieces into their apartment. The psychic said that she had a talk with the grandmother and there were no more disturbances.

DAYTON COUNTRY CLUB

Established in 1897, the Dayton Country Club is the oldest continuously operating club west of the Alleghenies. Sounds of a party can be heard at night when the club is empty. Glasses clinking, music and voices can all be heard but when anyone goes to look, nothing is seen.

15

UNMASKING URBAN LEGENDS

*U**rban legend**:* a humorous or horrific story or piece of information circulated as though true, especially one purporting to involve someone vaguely related or known to the teller.

Some stories are simply that—stories. While many ghost stories have roots in an event or have historical significance, many simply appear one day and propel themselves forward. What follows are local examples of stories that do not have roots.

CARPENTER ROAD

A small countryside street located in Sugarcreek Township, this road appears innocuous and quiet, but it has played host to many stories for ghost hunters and daring teens over the years.

The most common story involves a family living in one of the houses in the area that fell victim to a murder-suicide many years ago. The father, an avid drinker, went "crazy" one night and killed his entire family, including the family pets, using an axe from his barn. On foggy nights, he is said to be seen walking the field near his former home, still carrying the axe used to butcher his family.

Many of the stories from this street took place at the bend in the road. (This bend no longer exists; a housing development has since been built.) A man supposedly hanged himself from one of the trees and his shadow can be seen walking in the grass in that area—sometimes a moan or two can be heard on a still night. Also on the bend is the "witch's house." There is not much information or legend about this, just the firm assertion that it does, in fact, exist. If one dared to stop their car on the bend, which was practically a ninety-degree turn, legend has it that the car would not start again.

WITCH'S STEPS, AKA THIRTEEN STEPS TO HELL

If you visit Canal Lock Park near the corner of Endicott Road and Fishburg Road in Huber Heights, you will see a set of stone steps leading to nowhere. Where once stood a house, all that is left to show for it now are the steps, which are considered to be cursed or haunted. As the story goes, the nearby townspeople stormed down Fishburg to the house of a suspected witch and burned her to death in front of her home. As she burned, she angrily cursed the land and the steps the townspeople ran up to get to her. After her death, her spirit remained behind. If you stand at the steps and listen quietly, you can hear the sound of her deranged laughter. Reportedly, a satanic cult practiced at this site, believing the witch's death made it sacred. If you choose to walk the steps, you will notice twelve steps on the way up but thirteen steps going down. Watch your step as you walk down, because you may feel a set of hands pushing you from behind.

STONER PARK

The legend of a retirement home whose residents participated in a mass suicide is attributed to Beavercreek. According to urban legend, the residents locked themselves in the building and set fire to the clothing they wore. The building and residents burned completely. During the fall season, as you walk the path in the woods you can see the glowing forms of humans running in the distance and hear mysterious sounds.

It's an interesting story, but there was no retirement home mass suicide. There is not even a Stoner Park in Beavercreek. The closest reference to a Stoner Park appears in a 1905 article in the *Dayton Herald* mentioning a farmer's picnic at Stoner's Park, "four miles north of the city."

Witch's Steps, located in Huber Heights.

LOVER'S LANE / HOOKMAN

The Lover's Lane / Hookman story dates in popularity to around the 1950s. It grew in reputation when a version of it was published in the advice column Dear Abby. The common aspect of the legend involves teenagers parking a car somewhere to make out. In some versions, both teens stay in the car and hear scraping noises outside. Spooked, they decide to leave, only to later find a hook dangling from the door handle. Or they find deep scrapes along the side of the car. In various versions of the story that have circulated, one or both of the teens has been murdered or had a confrontation of sorts with the killer. Usually, the killer is an escaped convict or mental patient.

Perhaps the influence of these stories started in 1946, with a series of murders in Texarkana (the area of Texas, Arkansas, Louisiana) known as the Texarkana Moonlight Murders. The attacks were made on male-female couples who sought privacy in Lover's Lane settings, such as secluded roads or an abandoned barn. The Texarkana Moonlight Murderer was never caught, which easily launched the story less than a decade later when the hookman story was published in Dear Abby.

Whether the urban legend was propelled forward because of the Texarkana murders or because of Dear Abby, parents used it to deter their teens from going parking at night, convincing them it was dangerous to do so.

The Forney Road Hookman is Dayton's contribution to this legend. Teens in Germantown and New Lebanon have been warned not to go parking on that road at night because the Hookman lies in wait. If you park on Forney Road, an old man with a hook for a hand will run out from the woods and chase you away. Rumors of a biker gang dumping bodies have also circulated.

Other nearby locations with a version of this legend include Pond Run Road in Cincinnati and the legend of Enos Kay on Egypt Road in Chillicothe.

CRYBABY BRIDGE

There are various versions of Crybaby Bridge, but common to every version of the story is the sound of a baby crying. Commonly, the story involves a car accident with the mother driving and she and her baby go over the bridge and do not survive. Other versions tell of a suicide or murder, always involving the death of the baby and one of the parents, usually the mother. A ghostly mother can often be seen or heard walking the area near the bridge, searching for her lost baby.

Dayton has many versions of this story, one of which is set on Hyde Road in Yellow Springs. If you park, you can hear a baby crying and the sound of the baby's mother running around the bridge. Footprints will appear on your car if you stay still long enough. Legend states that the mother killed her baby before taking her own life. In Xenia, a father supposedly dropped his baby into the river. When near the bridge, people have reported hearing strange sounds, feeling watched and even seeing apparitions on Wilberforce Clifton Road. At James Barber Road Bridge, a fisherman supposedly pulled out a skeleton of a baby and ever since, the sound of a baby crying can be heard.

Other local versions of this story are set in Magee Park in Bellbrook (the bridge is no longer there) and on Maud Hughes Road in Liberty Township. Both of these crybaby legends involve a woman getting pregnant outside of marriage. Maud Hughes Bridge is also referred to as the Screaming Bridge because of a train accident near that bridge in 1909. Screams filled the air as the injured waited to be rescued. It is said their pained screams can still be heard today.

GHOSTLY BRIDES

There are countless versions of the Ghostly Bride legend. The one constant is the bride dying in her wedding dress or on her wedding day. In some stories, her groom left her before the wedding, leaving her heartbroken and refusing to take off the dress. One such story involves Esther Hale from Doylestown, Ohio. Esther refused to take her dress off and died several months later still wearing the dress. One popular version of the Ghostly Bride story has the bride playing hide-and-seek with the wedding party. She hides in an old trunk in an attic. The trunk lid gets stuck and the bride is trapped inside. She isn't found for a few years until someone cleans out the attic and opens the trunk to find her mummified remains. In others versions, she dies on the way to or from the church.

Our local version of this story has the bride getting ready at home. The mother, brother and sister of the bride are at the church decorating and greeting guests. The father of the bride waits patiently for his little girl to finish getting ready so he can take her to the church. As most do, this bride takes a long time to get ready for her big day. After she puts on her dress, which was her grandmother's, and finishes her last touches, she asks her father to hurry getting her to the church.

Quickly, she climbs into the buggy at the time she was supposed to be at the church and before she sits down, they are off. They take off down Trebein Road near Byron. She is still adjusting her veil as her father urges the horse to go faster over the bumps and dips in the road. The dusty road is not forgiving as they race to the church. The buggy hits a rock in the road and the poor girl goes flying out of the buggy. She hits the ground hard and breaks her neck. She is killed instantly.

The next day, her father and the groom return to the place in the road where the accident happened and dig the very large rock out. They throw it onto the side of the road where it remains to this day. Two days after the accident, they bury the bride in her grandmother's wedding dress in a cemetery less than a mile from the accident.

These days, she can be seen as a vision in white crossing Trebein Road, often spotted near midnight on an August night. She is described as ethereal or misty. Some have seen her full appearance, looking like a real person. In some cases, drivers have stopped to see if she needs help only to see her disappear. In each case, she appears to be trying to get to the church to meet her groom. Some say that if you encounter the bride and she touches you, you will become old and she will be young and alive again.

HAUNTED SCHOOLS

Haunted schools generally involve a story about a former student or teacher who continues to haunt the school. If the story revolves around a teacher, it's usually a story of a teacher murdered. A student death is usually a suicide due to academic pressure. In all versions of the story, the death occurs under mysterious circumstances and the ghost continues to haunt the classrooms and hallways.

The Dayton area has many examples of this, including one involving Beavercreek High School. As the story goes, a teacher was murdered there and continues to haunt the school. She is particularly cruel to female students, because a girl murdered her. Another example is Spring Hill Elementary in Xenia. The school is haunted by the ghost of a former teacher murdered over one hundred years ago. A translucent white apparition roams the grounds and the locals believe it's the teacher looking for her murderer.

Oakwood High School boasts a pair of haunts as well, with a former student who committed suicide in the junior hallway in the 1960s or 1970s. Students have seen fleeting glimpses of his ghost along with hearing his footsteps throughout the school. The other haunting involves a young woman but it is not known if she was a student or a resident of the house that was on the land before the school was built. She is also seen in the junior hallway and has been seen sitting on a bench after the school is closed.

Other local haunted schools include Valley View High School in Germantown, where a young student was killed in a car accident and haunts the former band room. Music has been heard coming from the room when it is empty. Lockers open and close on their own, as does the locker room door. Medlar View Elementary in Miamisburg is said to be haunted by a young girl who was murdered by a construction worker. She can be seen in the reflection in the mirror. It is not said why, but anyone seeing her ghost is warned not to talk to her. A strange moaning sound can be heard at Baker Middle School in Fairborn. That ghost is also said to shake desks and haunt the gym and surrounding classrooms.

BIBLIOGRAPHY

1. Dayton's Blessing from the Watervliet Shakers

Gurvis, Sandra. *Myths and Mysteries of Ohio: True Stories of the Unsolved and Unexplained.* Guilford, CT: Globe Pequot, 2014.

Ohio History Central. "Shakers." Accessed August 12, 2022. https://ohiohistorycentral.org.

Remarkable Ohio. Accessed July 22, 2022. https://remarkableohio.org.

Shea, John Gerald. *The American Shakers and Their Furniture, with Measured Drawings of Museum Classics.* New York: Van Nostrand Reinhold Company, 1971.

2. Ghostly Graveyards

Boyer, Cassidy. "The 10 Most Haunted Places in Dayton." *Dayton (OH) Daily News*, 2022.

City of Miamisburg. "Hillgrove Union Cemetery." December 9, 2021. https://cityofmiamisburg.com.

Dayton Journal, August 17, 1860.

Deitering, Joyce. "The Ghosts of Dayton." Oldham & Deitering, October 29, 2021. https://www.gemcitylaw.com.

Historic Woodland Cemetery & Arboretum. *The Boy & Dog* (monument). Johnny Morehouse tombstone. Dayton, Ohio.

Kachuba, John B. *Ghosthunting Ohio.* Cincinnati, OH: Emmis Books, 2004.

Paul. "October 29, 2013." Redneck Latte Ravings. Accessed August 20, 2022. https://www.rednecklatte.com.

Stansfield, Charles A. *Haunted Ohio: Ghosts and Strange Phenomena of the Buckeye State*. Guilford, CT: Globe Pequot, 2019.

Weatherly, David. "Haunted Woodland Cemetery, Dayton, Ohio." Eerie Lights, October 24, 2019. www.eerielights.com.

Willis, James. *The Big Book of Ohio Ghost Stories*. Mechanicsburg, PA: Stackpole Books, 2013.

Woodyard, Chris. *Haunted Ohio*. Beavercreek, OH: Kestrel, 1991.

———. *Haunted Ohio IV*. Beavercreek, OH: Kestrel, 1997.

3. Bizarre Beasts

Benedict, Adam. "Cryptid Profile: The Crosswick Monster." Pine Barrens Institute, October 15, 2020. https://pinebarrensinstitute.com.

Cisneros, Jenna. "13 Ohio Counties Now Confirming Cases of 'Zombie Deer.'" WRGT, September 1, 2022. www.dayton247now.com.

Cook, Joedy. Interview with author, Dayton, Ohio, August 27, 2022.

Dayton Daily News. "More Dayton Urban (and Rural) Legends." February 24, 1997.

Dogman Encounters. "Want to Learn More about Dogman Encounters? Well, You've Come to the Right Place!" June 16, 2021. https://dogmanencounters.com.

Igo, Harold. *Haunted House: Spooky Tales of Yellow Springs*. Yellow Springs, MD: Yellow Springs Historical Society, 1943.

Lepper, Brad. "Archaeology: Newspapers Have Been Debunking Giant Hoaxes for a Long Time." *Columbus Dispatch*, December 27, 2020.

Warren County Historical Society. "Crosswick Snake Monster." August 14, 2020. https://www.wchsmuseum.org.

Weird Ohio. Accessed August 30, 2022. www.weirdusa.com/states/ohio.

4. Dreadful Deaths

Dayton Herald. "Was She Murdered?" September 4, 1896.

Dayton Unknown. "Bess Little." May 20, 2016. www.daytonunknown.com.

Golden Lamb. "Our Story." Accessed August 25, 2022. www.goldenlamb.com.

Greene County Archives. "Spooky Tales from the Greene County Archives: Facts and Myths behind Harold Igo's Ghost Stories." YouTube, November 2, 2020. Video, 59:01. www.youtube.com.

Gurvis, Sandra. *Myths and Mysteries of Ohio: True Stories of the Unsolved and Unexplained*. Guilford, CT: Globe Pequot, 2014.

Heise, Robin. "Double Murder in Yellow Springs." Yellow Springs Heritage, October 21, 2014. https://ysheritage.org.

Kachuba, John B. *Ghosthunting Ohio*. Cincinnati, OH: Emmis Books, 2004.
————. *Ghosthunting Ohio: On the Road Again*. Cincinnati, OH: Emmis Books, 2011.
Mudcat Café. "Lyr Req: My Pretty Quadroon." Accessed August 22, 2022. https://mudcat.org.
National Police Gazette. "Murder or Suicide?" January 16, 1897.
Reddit. "Morningstar Rd, Carlisle—One of Our Many Haunted Roads. Happy October." Accessed August 30, 2022. www.reddit.com.
San Francisco Examiner. "The Mysterious Murder of Bessie Little." October 4, 1896.
Willis, James. *The Big Book of Ohio Ghost Stories*. Mechanicsburg, PA: Stackpole Books, 2013.
Woodyard, Chris. *Haunted Ohio II*. Beavercreek, OH: Kestrel, 1992.
Xenia (OH) Daily Gazette. "Fatal Thirteen." January 27, 1897.

5. Eerie Eateries

Bachman, Megan. "Tales of Hauntings in the Village." *Yellow Springs (OH) News*, November 3, 2010.
Dayton.com. "Spooky Eats: The Most Haunted Restaurants in Dayton." October 14, 2021. https://www.dayton.com.
Dray, April. "The Oldest Bar in Ohio Has a Fascinating History." Only In Your State, May 22, 2018. https://www.onlyinyourstate.com.
The Florentine Restaurant. "Our Story." Accessed August 26, 2022. https://www.theflorentinerestaurant.com.
Greene County Ohio. "Out of the Clock Tower." October 25, 2018. www.greenecountyohio.gov.
Kachuba, John B. *Ghosthunting Ohio*. Cincinnati, OH: Emmis Books, 2004.
Rowe, Rosella C. "Bennett's Publical Family Sports Grill." *My Haunted Travel Blog!*, May 25, 2020. https://myhauntedtravelblog.blogspot.com.
Walsh, Andrew. "Schnitzel, Pierogi, and Ghosts? The Amber Rose in Old North Dayton." Dayton Vistas, January 27, 2018. https://daytonvistas.com.

6. Supernatural Stages

Butler County Connect. "Middletown's First Multi-Millionaire…A Story of Collaboration." Accessed August 21, 2022. www.butlercountyconnect.com.
Dayton (OH) Daily News. "People Pay Public Honor." May 27, 1902.
Dayton Local. "Memories of Blue Jacket Drama." Accessed August 21, 2022. https://www.daytonlocal.com.

GhostQuest.net. "Haunted Ohio." Accessed August 20, 2022. www. ghostquest.net.

Gurvis, Sandra. *Myths and Mysteries of Ohio: True Stories of the Unsolved and Unexplained.* Guilford, CT: Globe Pequot, 2014.

Huffman, Dale. "Ghost Search Yields Faint Results." *Dayton Daily News*, October 20, 1970.

Paul. "October 29, 2013." Redneck Latte Ravings. Accessed August 20, 2022. https://www.rednecklatte.com.

The Searchlight (Redding, CA). "Lillian Graham Disappears Causing a Stage Sensation." July 26, 1911.

Thay, Edrick. *Ghost Stories of Ohio.* Tukwila, WA: Lone Pine Publishing, 2002.

True Ghost Tales. "The Sorg Opera House Ghosts." Accessed August 21, 2022. www.trueghosttales.com.

Washington Township. "About Town Hall Theatre." Accessed August 21, 2022. https://www.washingtontwp.org.

Wikipedia. "Blue Jacket." Accessed May 16, 2022. www.wikipedia.org.

———. "Paul J. Sorg." Accessed July 3, 2022. www.wikipedia.org.

Wikiwand. "Town Hall Theatre (Centerville)." Accessed August 21, 2022. www.wikiwand.com.

Woodyard, Chris. *Ghost Hunter's Guide to Haunted Ohio.* Beavercreek, OH: Kestrel, 2000.

———. *Haunted Ohio.* Beavercreek, OH: Kestrel, 1991.

7. Enduring Entities

Montgomery County Common Pleas Court. "The Old Montgomery County Courthouse." www.montcourt.oh.gov.

Peterson, Skip. "R.H. Grant: Selling Chevrolet." *Journal News* (Hamilton, OH), November 29, 2011.

Wikimapia. "Normandy United Methodist Church (former estate)." Accessed August 25, 2022. www.wikimapia.org.

Wikipedia. "East Second Street Historic District (Xenia, Ohio)." June 12, 2022. www.wikipedia.org.

Woodyard, Chris. *Haunted Ohio II.* Beavercreek, OH: Kestrel, 1992.

———. *Haunted Ohio IV.* Beavercreek, OH: Kestrel, 1997.

———. *The Headless Horror: Strange and Ghostly Ohio Tales.* Beavercreek, OH: Kestrel, 2013.

8. Phantom Phenomena

Delphos (OH) Courant. "Phantom Returns to Highways." March 29, 1952.

Delphos (OH) Daily Herald. "Grim Skeleton Rides Highways." March 8, 1952.

Evening Review (East Liverpool, OH). "Highway Ghost Phones Warning of Tonight's Run." March 28, 1952.

———. "His Name Is Legion." March 18, 1952.

———. "No Report on Phantom. Maybe He's Lost in Fog." March 31, 1952.

Greenville (OH) Daily Advocate. "Highway 'Ghost' Is Seen Again; Creates Prosecution Puzzle." March 10, 1952.

———. "Phantom Appears." April 1, 1952.

———. "Phantom Challenges Sheriff to 'Spook Race'." March 15, 1952.

Heck, E.L. "Tales and Sketches of the Great Miami Valley." Unpublished manuscript, 1962.

Marysville (OH) Journal-Tribune. "Four Motorists See 'Phantom'." March 28, 1952.

Ohio State Highway Patrol. "About OSHP." Accessed July 14, 2022. https://statepatrol.ohio.gov.

Salem News (Lisbon, OH). "Frightened Drivers Glimpse Route 40 Driver in Area." March 27, 1952.

Sandusky (OH) Register. "Route 40 Phantom." March 7, 1952.

Times Recorder (Zanesville, OH). "Highway Phantom Shifts Location." March 14, 1952.

———. "Marshall Challenges 'Phantom'." March 20, 1952.

———. "Takes Latest Scientific Gadgets for Successful Ghosts These Days." March 15, 1952.

9. Mysterious Matters

Bachman, Megan. "Tales of Hauntings in the Village." *Yellow Springs (OH) News,* November 3, 2010. https://ysnews.com.

Capital Punishment UK. "Hanged by the Neck until You Are Dead! (USA)." Accessed August 25, 2022. http://www.capitalpunishmentuk.org.

Dayton Daily Journal, October 11, 1870.

Democrat and Chronicle (Rochester, NY). "This Beats a Tattooed Man." August 31, 1903.

Elam, Phillip. "Xenia Tornado of 1974." Out of the Box, February 26, 2019. https://blogs.libraries.wright.edu/news/outofthebox.

Gallipolis Journal, October 27, 1870.

Halasz, Scott. "Xenia Tornado Remembered 46 Years Later." *Xenia (OH) Gazette,* April 3, 2020. https://www.xeniagazette.com.

Princeton (IN) Daily Clarion. "Little Child Is Human Book; Bible Verses Appear on Body." September 4, 1903.

Tucson Daily Citizen. September 28, 1904.

Woodyard, Chris. *Haunted Ohio*. Beavercreek, OH: Kestrel, 1991.

———. *Haunted Ohio II*. Beavercreek, OH: Kestrel, 1992.

10. School Spirits

Deitering, Joyce. "The Ghosts of Dayton." Oldham & Deitering, October 29, 2021. https://www.gemcitylaw.com.

Ghostly World. "University of Dayton, Ghostly World." Accessed August 24, 2022. https://www.ghostlyworld.org.

Ohio Exploration Society. "Stivers Middle School—Contribution." May 22, 2016. https://www.ohioexploration.com.

Sinclair Community College. Accessed August 21, 2022. http://www.sinclair.edu.

University of Dayton Magazine. "Truth or Tale." September 13, 2019. https://udayton.edu.

Woodyard, Chris. *Haunted Ohio*. Beavercreek, OH: Kestrel, 1991.

———. *Haunted Ohio II*. Beavercreek, OH: Kestrel, 1992

———. *Haunted Ohio IV*. Beavercreek, OH: Kestrel, 1997.

11. Paranormal Parks

Bartiromo, Michael. "These States Have More 'Credible' Bigfoot Sightings than Others, According to Bigfoot Investigators." News Nation, August 27, 2022. www.newsnationnow.com.

Five Rivers MetroParks. "Englewood Metropark." December 1, 2021. www.metroparks.org.

Frederick (MD) Daily News. "Real Live Ghost." March 27, 1884.

Ghosts of America. "Bellbrook, Ohio Ghost Sightings, Page 5." Accessed August 25, 2022. http://www.ghostsofamerica.com.

Higgins, Ray. "Tales of Haunted House Recalled by Observance." *Xenia (OH) Daily Gazette*, June 18, 1966.

Howe, Linda Moulton. "Update on Miamisburg, Ohio, Corn Pictogram: Balls of Light?" Earth Files. Accessed July 16, 2022. www.earthfiles.com.

Ledger Independent (Maysville, KY). "Soybean Field a Bit Too Popular since Design Discovered." March 8, 2018. https://maysville-online.com.

Ohio History Connection. "Miamisburg Mound." Accessed May 19, 2022. www.ohiohistory.org.

Prodigy Paranormal Group. "Patty Family Homestead." Accessed September 2, 2022. www.theprodigygroup.org.

Project Paranormal. "Bigfoot Encounter Magee Park Bellbrook Ohio, PPI 10-27-11." YouTube. March 1, 2013. Video, 13:00. https://www.youtube.com.

Scribd. "The Earl Miller Monkey House." Accessed November 3, 2022. https://www.scribd.com.

Sherman, Mary. "Ghosts & Legends of Bellbrook" (unpublished manuscript). Bellbrook, Ohio, 1981.

The Tolle Road, ed. "The Miamisburg Crop Circle." YouTube, June 18, 2014. Video, 26:12. https://www.youtube.com.

Vandalia Ohio. "Helke Park." Accessed August 26, 2022. www.vandaliaohio.org.

Wilson, Jeff. "New Crop Circle, Miamisburg Mound in Miamisburg, Ohio." Rense. Accessed July 17, 2022. www.rense.com.

Woodyard, Chris. *Haunted Ohio II*. Beavercreek, OH: Kestrel, 1992

Xenia (OH) Daily Gazette. "Bellbrook Girl Thought Killed by Lightning." May 18, 1967.

———. "A Tribute to Peggy." May 27, 1967.

12. Haunted Houses

Air & Space Forces Magazine. "Namesakes: Wright-Patterson." January 21, 2022. https://www.airforcemag.com.

Cincinnati (OH) Enquirer. "Angry Ghosts." February 2, 1892.

Fulmer, Chesta. "'Ghosts' Fail to Daunt One Female Reporter." *Dayton (OH) Journal*, September 1, 1938.

"Patterson Homestead" sign. Patterson Homestead, Dayton, Ohio. Viewed August 8, 2022.

Schlosser, S.E. *Spooky Ohio: Tales of Hauntings, Strange Happenings, and Other Local Lore*. Guilford, CT: Globe Pequot Press, 2021.

Wikipedia. "Berryhill-Morris House." June 1, 2022. www.wikipedia.org.

———. "Hawthorn Hill." June 1, 2022. www.wikipedia.org.

Wikiwand. "Frank Stuart Patterson." Accessed August 24, 2022. www.wikiwand.com.

Willis, James *The Big Book of Ohio Ghost Stories* Mechanicsburg, PA: Stackpole Books, 2013.

Woodyard, Chris. *Ghost Hunter's Guide to Haunted Ohio*. Beavercreek, OH: Kestrel, 2000.

———. *Haunted Ohio*. Beavercreek, OH: Kestrel, 1991.

———. *Haunted Ohio V*. Beavercreek, OH: Kestrel, 2003.

Wright Brothers Aeroplane Co. "Wright Family." Accessed August 22, 2022. www.wrightbrothers.org.

13. Weird Wright-Patterson

Airplanes Online. "B-24 Liberator Strawberry Bitch." Accessed August 25, 2022. www.airplanes-online.com.

AvStop Magazine Online. "Sikorsky UH-19B Chickasaw." Accessed August 25, 2022. http://avstop.com.

Gurvis, Sandra. *Myths and Mysteries of Ohio: True Stories of the Unsolved and Unexplained*. Guilford, CT: Globe Pequot Press, 2014.

Kachuba, John B. *Ghosthunting Ohio*. Cincinnati, OH: Emmis Books, 2004.

National Museum of the United States Air Force. "Lady Be Good." Accessed August 25, 2022. www.nationalmuseum.af.mil.

National UFO Reporting Center. "International UFO Report Index." 2022. http://www.nuforc.org.

Pruitt, Sarah. "Does Hangar 18, Legendary Alien Warehouse, Exist?" History.com. January 17, 2020. www.history.com.

Ramsey, Scott, and Susan Ramsey. "Aztec UFO Crash Site." Explore Aztec. UFO Crash Site, March 25, 2007. www.aztecnm.com.

Stansfield, Charles A. *Haunted Ohio: Ghosts and Strange Phenomena of the Buckeye State*. Guilford, CT: Globe Pequot Press, 2019.

Stilwell, Blake. "6 Urban Legends about Wright-Patterson Air Force Base." We Are the Mighty, September 2, 2021. www.wearethemighty.com.

The Tolle Road. "Haunted Air Force Museum—Dayton, OH." YouTube, October 23, 2020. Video, 13:14. https://www.youtube.com.

United States Air Force. "Henry. H. Arnold." Accessed September 8, 2022. https://www.af.mil.

USAF Rotorheads. "Black Mariah." December 31, 2015. http://www.rotorheadsrus.us.

Wikipedia. "Aztec, New Mexico UFO Hoax." August 13, 2022. www.wikipedia.org.

———. "Project Blue Book." Accessed June 1, 2022. www.wikipedia.org.

14. Terrifying Tidbits

Dayton (OH) Daily News. "Ghost Stories Haunt Close to Home." October 31, 2002.

Defiance (OH) Democrat, February 15, 1873

Gurvis, Sandra. *Myths and Mysteries of Ohio: True Stories of the Unsolved and Unexplained*. Guilford, CT: Globe Pequot Press, 2014.

Igo, Harold. *Haunted House: Spooky Tales of Yellow Springs*. Yellow Springs, MD: Yellow Springs Historical Society, 1943.

Kachuba, John B. *Ghosthunting Ohio, On the Road Again.* Cincinnati, OH: Emmis Books, 2011.

Ohio Exploration Society. "Hauntings & Legends of Ohio." February 5, 2017. https://www.ohioexploration.com.

Schlosser, S.E. *Spooky Ohio: Tales of Hauntings, Strange Happenings, and Other Local Lore.* Guilford, Connecticut: Globe Pequot Press, 2021.

Sherman, Mary. "Ghosts & Legends of Bellbrook." Unpublished manuscript. Bellbrook, Ohio, 1981.

Woodyard, Chris. *The Face in the Window: Haunting Ohio Tales.* Beavercreek, OH: Kestrel, 2013.

———. *Haunted Ohio.* Beavercreek, OH: Kestrel, 1991.

———. *The Headless Horror: Strange and Ghostly Ohio Tales.* Beavercreek, OH: Kestrel, 2013.

Woodyard, Chris, and Jessica Wiesel. *Spooky Ohio: 13 Traditional Tales.* Beavercreek, OH: Kestrel, 1995.

15. Unmasking Urban Legends

Dayton Convention and Visitors Bureau. "Haunted Dayton: The Most Haunted Places in Montgomery County." October 21, 2020. www.daytoncvb.com.

Dayton (OH) Herald. "Farmers Picnic," August 2, 1905.

GhostQuest.net. "Haunted Ohio." Accessed August 20, 2022. www.ghostquest.net.

Ohio Exploration Society. "Greene County Hauntings & Legends." October 2, 2016. https://www.ohioexploration.com.

Woodyard, Chris. *Haunted Ohio III.* Beavercreek, OH: Kestrel, 1994.

ABOUT THE AUTHOR

Sara Kaushal was born and raised in a suburb of Dayton, Ohio, and lives in another suburb of Dayton in a ghost-free house with her husband, Ravindu, and their son Yuvi. Sara is a Dayton historian and the author of *Murder & Mayhem in Dayton and the Miami Valley* and the primary author of the blog *Dayton Unknown*. Sara can't drive through Dayton without pointing out at least one haunted place. She loves true crime, mysteries and ghost stories. She has a bookshelf full of books she intends to read one day.